# THE CONTEMPLATIVE EXPERIENCE

*A Blessing*

I gladly welcome this little work of Fr. Joseph Chu-Cong, a Trappist monk. The writer intended primarily to address his fellow brothers; his simple message, however, can be of interest to others too. It is the sharing of some contemplative experience which the writer obtained from his spiritual reading. It is a small work, but it expresses some deep biblical insight and the subtlety of Oriental wisdom. Here the spiritual masters of both East and West meet in the "Ground of their being," united to one another in a wonderful way. The understanding of the message can serve as a point of departure for the East–West dialogue that has been inaugurated and encouraged by the Second Vatican Council and the Bishop's Conference of the Philippines.

It has been said that men and women of our times have been interested in exploring their inner world, in their deepest Self. This little work serves as a finger that points the way to that "inner world." It can be an even better opportunity for those people who, like most of the Asian people, are born "contemplative."

To this modest work I gladly give my blessing, wishing that it might become like a mustard seed which grows and becomes a tree for the birds of the air to come and breathe, or like the yeast a woman took and mixed in with three measures of flour until it was leavened all through.

*James Cardinal Sin, D.D.*
*Archbishop of Manila*

# The Contemplative Experience

*Erotic Love and Spiritual Union*

Joseph Chu-Cong, O.C.S.O.

*Introduction*

*by*

*The Rev. Cynthia Bourgeault, Ph.D.*

A Crossroad Book
The Crossroad Publishing Company
New York

The Crossroads Publishing Company
www.CrossroadPublishing.com

Printed in the United States of America

**Library of Congress Cataloging-in-Publication Data**

Chu-Cong, Joseph.
    The contemplative experience : erotic love and spiritual union /
  Joseph Chu-Cong : introduction by Cynthia Bourgeault.
       p.      cm.
     ISBN 0-8245-1781-4
     1. Contemplation.   2. Erotica–Religious aspects–Christianity.
  I. Title.
  BV5091.C7C48    1999
  248.3' 4–dc21                                        99-15980
                                                       CIP

This printing: 2017

To JAMES CARDINAL SIN, Archbishop of Manila, who bestowed his paternal blessings on this humble work; to Dom Bernardo Olivera, who kindly wrote the preface; to Fr. Thomas Keating and Dr. Cynthia Bourgeault, who gave birth to this revised edition.

To MY FELLOW CISTERCIANS of both Branches, particularly my brothers at St. Joseph's Abbey in Spencer; to my fellow priests and religious both men and women everywhere. I would like to remind them that in order to preserve the integrity of our commitments we need to establish, with the grace of God, our intimacy with Our Lord Jesus Christ, an intimacy as overwhelming as the intimacy of a man with a woman, and that of a woman with a man.

LAST BUT NOT LEAST, TO ALL MARRIED PEOPLE. I like to tell them that marriage is a sacrament of great power, of beauty, and of sanctity. Their ecstatic conjugal union is in no way an obstacle to their friendship with God. When they are deeply together they should have God in between. At the wedding of Great Britain's Princess Elizabeth, the Archbishop of Canterbury spoke to the royal couple:

> The everlasting Christ is here to bless you.
> The nearer you keep to Him,
> the nearer you will be to one another.

To THOSE READERS who would ordinarily shrink from the words "intimate union," or "erotic love," skip those sections if you care to. However, I would like to ask you not to be hesitant. Take courage—and fear not to embark on the contemplative journey which I have attempted to describe in these pages.

# Contents

## PART FOUR
### CONTEMPLATIVE EXPERIENCE AND BEYOND

## PART FIVE
### EPILOGUE

# Acknowledgments

THE 1990 CISTERCIAN GENERAL CHAPTER in Rome inspired me to write these essays. They first took shape as a small book called *Contemplative Experience*, published in the Philippines, where I served for eight years as Titular Prior and then as Abbot of Our Lady of the Philippines Monastery.

Dom Thomas Keating, former abbot of St. Joseph's Abbey, presented the first version of my book to Mrs. Lynn Quinn, his editor at Crossroad, who kindly suggested that I revise it with a view to addressing the general public. Dr. Cynthia Bourgeault has edited this revision with great insight and unlimited patience and kindly wrote the introduction. Fr. Gerald Sears, our computer technician here at St. Joseph's Abbey, has been patient and kind in helping me to set the manuscript on my word processor. The monastery's librarians have helped me to locate the sources I needed; Br. Meinrad retyped the corrected manuscript; and Fr. Basil Pennington read proofs of the book.

I would like to acknowledge the editors and publishers of the writings of the Cistercian Fathers whom I have quoted, particularly St. Bernard of Clairvaux. Whenever possible, I have tried to give accurate references and quotations when using their material.

Concerning the "sayings" and anecdotes of the Asian non-Christian masters, I take the liberty of not giving detailed references. This is mainly because I do not intend this work to be a scholarly study in this field. These sayings are more like the *Apophthegmata* of our Western masters. They have become like axioms or proverbs; they are so familiar to those acquainted with the Oriental tradition that such an apparatus would probably sound tedious or contrived. The sayings are pearls of wisdom that belong to everyone and are found on almost every page of the literature.

The author and the publisher wish to acknowledge with gratitude permission to use within this book excerpts from previously published material.

Excerpts from *Sermons of St. Bernard of Clairvaux on the Song of Songs* in four volumes, translated by Kilian Walsh. Copyright © 1971, 1980, 1983, 1993 by Cistercian Publications, Kalamazoo, Michigan. Reprinted by permission of the publisher.

Excerpts from *The Foundations of Mysticism* by Bernard McGinn. Copyright © 1991, by Bernard McGinn, published by The Crossroad Publishing Company, New York. Reprinted by permission of the publisher.

Excerpts from *Eros and Allegory*, by Denys Turner. Copyright © 1995 by Cistercian Publications. Reprinted by permission of the publisher.

Excerpts from *Meister Eckhart: Mystic and Philosopher*, by Reiner Schumann. Copyright © 1978 by Indiana University Press. Reprinted by permission of the publisher.

Excerpts from *Souls of Fire: Portraits and Legends of Hasidic Masters*, by Elie Wiesel. Copyright © 1972 by Georges Borchardt, Inc. Reprinted by permission of Georges Borchardt, Inc.

Excerpt from *The Zen Koan*, by Isshu Miura and Ruth Fuller Sasaki. Copyright © 1965 by Harcourt Brace Publishers. Reprinted by permission of the publisher.

The five diagrams by Erich Fromm from *Zen Buddhism & Psychoanalysis*, by D. T. Suzuki and Erich Fromm. Copyright ©

1960 by The Zen Studies Society, Inc. Diagrams copyright ©
1960 by Erich Fromm. "The Human Situation and Zen Buddhism." All rights reserved. For information address Harper &
Row, Publishers, Inc., 49 East 33d Street, New York, New York
10016.

Excerpt from *Zen Comments on the Mumonkan,* translated by
Sumiko Kudo. Copyright © 1975 by New American Library.

Every effort has been made to reach the rightful owners of
copyrighted material. If for any reason we have inadvertently
omitted acknowledgment of any copyright holder, please notify
The Crossroad Publishing Company for correction in any future
printings.

To all the good people mentioned above, I am very grateful.

Joseph Chu-Cong, O.C.S.O.
Spencer, Massachusetts
June 8, 1999

# Foreword

IT GIVES ME JOY TO RECOMMEND *The Contemplative Experi-ence*. The reader may find in this essay a way of carrying out spiritual reading that leads to the encounter with Christ and intimate union with him.

The Holy Spirit still continues to animate us here and now, and Sacred Scripture is the place par excellence where Christ makes the church—his Bride—to taste, even now, the mysteries of the age to come.

It is appropriate that the writer reminded us of the challenge made by Thomas Merton when he invited us to articulate our own contemplative experience. This is what the people of God expect of us. This is in line with Sacred Scripture, which says, "It is right to keep the secret of a king, yet it is right to reveal and publish the works of God" (Tobit 12:7).

Bernardo Olivera, O.C.S.O.
Abbot General

# Introduction

AMONG THE MOST PROFOUND AND NOBLE expressions of Christian spirituality is the great tradition of monastic love mysticism, which flowed (straight from the heart of Christ, monks would say) like a luminous stream through the early centuries of the church and reached its full flowering in twelfth-century Cistercian monasticism in the inspired mystical writings of St. Bernard of Clairvaux. Steeped in the imagery of the biblical Song of Songs and the "bridal mysticism" of the early church, it celebrates a path where the power of erotic desire, purified and redirected to God, breaks through the heat of its own desiring into the fullness of Christlike love.

Understandably, for the nonmonastic contemplative encountering this tradition, it is inevitable that questions of translation and credibility will arise. Is this monastic eros really the same erotic desire experienced by noncelibates in sexual intimacy? How can something as blatantly sensual as the imagery of the Song of Songs have come to be viewed as the quintessential expression of monastic celibate love? Must flesh-and-blood experience be sublimated or allegorized away before "holy desire" can become a true spiritual path? And if so, where does that leave most of the rest of us?

All who have ever been troubled by these questions will find remarkable reassurance and straight answers in this surprising little book by Fr. Joseph Chu-Cong, an eighty-year-old Trappist monk of St. Joseph's Abbey in Spencer, Massachusetts. In the end, there is only one way to "get there," and Fr. Joseph encourages us to take it—to open one's heart more and more deeply. The Christian path to spiritual union through "embracing holy desire" may come in celibate and noncelibate versions, but underneath it is always the same gesture: the ever-deepening surrender of one's being to the transforming power of love. "God's love is at the heart of all human and sexual intimacy," Fr. Joseph proclaims in the very first chapter of his book, not with the "Methinks the lady doth protest too much" tones that dominate the usual monastic discussions of conjugal love, but with the spontaneous certainty of one who, by following his own path of love faithfully to its end, has come to experience the heart of Love itself.

There are many ways one might introduce Fr. Joseph (previous to this book his work has been known only in monastic circles), but probably the best is simply to say that he is "one who got there." A native of Vietnam, born into a family with deep Christian roots, he was educated in Vietnamese Catholic seminaries and ordained in 1948 in the midst of the political turmoil already dividing the country. Sent to the United States for postgraduate studies in 1954, he found himself exiled here by the outbreak of the Vietnam War, and while praying for discernment as to where God might be leading him, he experienced a sudden, profound call to the contemplative life. He entered St. Joseph's Abbey in 1961 and has been there ever since, serving his community in a variety of ways—as novice master for twenty years, as the first abbot of the Order's new foundation in the Philippines, and most recently as the prior of his home community in Spencer. His little book, reminding one in many ways of Br. Lawrence's *Practice of the Presence of God,* is the product of a lifetime's study, reflection, and experience walking the path.

"The 'moments' of contemplative experience are the golden moments when we experience ourselves as deeply loved . . . to the marrow of our bones," Fr. Joseph writes at the beginning of chapter 3 in part 1. With love as his touchstone, he guides the reader steadily along the path of contemplative experience—from its first upwellings in what might be called "mystical awakening" to its culmination in spiritual union, where the contemplative vision has become an abiding state of consciousness. Freely sharing his own struggles and breakthroughs along this path, he offers his readers the keys that have unlocked the doors for him and can unlock them for us as well. Modest in size though it may be, this little volume is the most honest, lucid, and practical "user's guide" to the vast tradition of Christian love mysticism I have yet seen. For those who have embarked on the Christian spiritual journey through a contemplative prayer group or monastic retreat and wish to immerse themselves more deeply in the treasures of the monastic tradition, this book is a continuing source of wisdom and encouragement.

Although a lifelong Christian, Fr. Joseph has learned deeply from the wisdom of the East (which, ironically, he first encountered as a monk at Spencer!). One of the most original and effective sections of the book is where he weaves together the "five stages of meditation" from Master Tozan Ryokai, a ninth-century Zen master, with the life and teachings of St. Bernard of Clairvaux to elucidate the deepening steps and stages in the journey to union. Beneath the disarming simplicity of Fr. Joseph's words and stories lies the subtle wisdom of a mature contemplative, which resonates all the more clearly the farther one advances along the path. This section is also a beautiful demonstration of how Christian metaphorical language works, and of the ways in which monks have allowed an enlightened heart to lead them beyond the literal meaning of a scriptural text to the unitive or "anagogical" treasure it holds. His chapter "Reading Scripture as Reading a Zen Koan" will be for many readers the most valuable in the book.

In its rich weaving of practical wisdom, scholarly insight, and lived experience, Fr. Joseph presents the traditional path of monastic love mysticism in a way that is credible, accessible, and inviting to contemporary men and women whose hearts long for a deeper and more intimate union with Christ. Whatever the circumstances of our lives, Fr. Joseph teaches us how to "embrace holy desire" and allow the very passion of that embrace to carry us to its fulfillment.

The Rev. Cynthia Bourgeault, Ph.D.

## PART ONE

# Contemplative Experience

### CHAPTER 1

# What Is Contemplative Experience?

THE SPARKLE OF LIFE AND THE DAILY WALK together, the life of friendship and of love—apply this in your relationship with God, and there you have the contemplative experience in its essence. In our daily faithfulness to love, whether it be in our walk with each other or with God, there are periods of dullness, but there are also the sparkles, the "high moments," the times of intimacy and communion. All belong to the contemplative experience.

Where do these contemplative moments take place? We have many examples of contemplative masters experiencing God in the setting of nature's wonders: Francis of Assisi, Bernard of Clairvaux, and the modern Zen master D. T. Suzuki, to name but a few. St. Francis's "Canticle of Brother Sun" is well known, as well as the stories of how he would scold the flowers, saying, "Be quiet! Be quiet! You speak of my Beloved. It is too much for me!"

Then there is St. Bernard, the twelfth-century mystic of the Cistercian Order, who was overcome when he realized that God permeates the whole of creation. His experience was that God is the "stone in the stones, the tree in the trees," and in the same way, the center point of his own soul. God resides at the heart of all that exists; from the most interior to the most visible, the whole world is "charged with the grandeur of God," in the words

3

of another, more recent contemplative poet, Gerard Manley Hopkins. To a close friend, Bernard confided his experience:

> Believe me as one who has experience, you will find much more among the woods than ever you will among books. Woods and stones will teach you what you can never hear from any master. Do you imagine you cannot suck honey from the rocks and oil from the hardest stone, that the mountains do not drop sweetness and the hills flow with milk and honey, that the valleys are not filled with corn? So many things occur to me which I could say to you that I can hardly restrain myself.[1]

It is not hard to imagine someone like Bernard, a monk immersed in the natural setting of a twelfth-century monastery, looking for and finding God in the natural world around him. The monastery of Citeaux was founded in a wild, marshy valley, and work on it had begun with the draining of the swamps. It was a harsh existence, but it brought the monks close to the earth and the elements. And in the very unforgivingness of the land and the harshness of the elements they came to know God speaking to them in a way that was fresh and intimate. As Shakespeare once said:

> Tongue in trees,
> Books in the running brooks,
> Sermons in stones
> And good in everything.
> —*As You Like It*, act 1, scene 2

It sounds as if *he* got the message. He probably did not get it from reading St. Bernard. Shakespeare probably never visited a monastery, but he "got it." We don't know much about his life, but it seems certain that he was no stranger to the contemplative experience; that is why he was able to craft words with elegance and profundity.

The Zen masters also delight in finding contemplative experience in the simple and natural elements of life. In the words of one of my favorite authors, D. T. Suzuki:

> When one's mind is religiously awakened, one feels as though in every blade of wild fern and solid stone there is something really transcending all human feelings, something which lifts one to be a real equal to that of heaven. One has a specific gift that detects something great in all the ordinary things of earth, something that transcends all quantitative measurement. He plunges himself into the very source of creativity and there drinks from life all that life has to give. He not only sees by taking a look, but he enters into the source of things and knows them at the point where our life receives its existence.[2]

This "point where our life receives its existence" is a dimensionless point and a timeless moment. It is always the same where it is found. When we awaken to the experience of "existence" itself, all the myriad forms of existence join in the chorus of love. No blade of grass or wild fern is too insignificant, and no moment is too ordinary to escape the dance of love that goes on in every particle of the earth whether we are awake to it or not. Their very existence is all that we need to know to be unlimited ourselves.

These "moments" come, I believe, to nearly all of us. For instance, how many have been inwardly moved by the sight of a morning glory blossoming in the fresh of the dawn, by the innocence of a child, or by the ecstatic beauty of conjugal love? In his book *The Presence of God,* Jean Cardinal Daniélou quotes a friend saying of her husband: "When I was close to him I nearly always had the sense of God's actual Presence."[3]

The following account of Philip Sheldrake in *Befriending Our Desires* is striking:

> Some years ago I was accompanying an older married man during his retreat. In his prayer he had been focusing on the image of the

potter in the opening verses of Jeremiah, chapter 18. "Yes, like clay in the potter's hand, so you are in mine, House of Israel." As he identified himself with the clay, the man found to his surprise that the thought of God's hands shaping him, especially re-forming him, was very frightening. We agreed that he should return to the same scripture passage in the course of the next day's prayer to see whether there should be any further enlightenment. Although it was unplanned and not his usual form of prayer, the man found himself visualizing the hands of God reaching out toward him. He tried honestly to invite God to shape him. But he could not do so; the experience still felt too threatening.

As he described it to me during our conversation the next day, he eventually gave up the struggle and simply sat blankly with himself, his fears and God. Quite unexpectedly the image of hands reaching out toward him returned. However, before he could once again recoil in fear, he saw that God's hands were the hands of his wife, which had caressed him so many times during their long marriage. It was a profound conversion experience on several levels. Clearly, something important about the man's fearful images of God was made explicit and healed in a substantial way. The man also took a step forward in the process of lowering his instinctive defenses and letting go in trust. However, most striking of all, the man understood that God's touch had been at the heart of all his human love and sexual intimacy.[4]

As I mentioned earlier, these moments of contemplative experience come to all of us. At the risk of being presumptuous, I would like to share one of my own humble "moments" with you. I am encouraged by the word of the angel Raphael to Tobit, "It is right to keep the secret of the king, yet it is right to reveal and publish the works of God" (Tobit 12:7).

My own contemplative experience is deeply connected to the mysteries of the Christian faith. It is in the realization of our human intimacy with God, and with Our Lord Jesus Christ, that I am personally inclined to locate the "highest moments" of my contemplative experience. Perhaps, then, a personal description of a prayer experience would not be out of place. I would like to show how even a slight taste of this experience brings with it a sense of joy that is always ineffable.

The antecedents to this particular experience were, first, my daily reading and meditating on the Word of God; second, my intense reading of St. Bernard's mystical writings; and, third, a period of intense reflection trying to "solve" a Zen koan, or riddle, which says:

> Empty hand, yet holding a hoe!
> Walking, yet riding a water buffalo![5]

For a long time I meditated on that koan. I asked myself, How can an empty hand hold anything? And how could a man walking on the ground experience himself riding? But as always with these koans, one "solves" the riddle when all the dualistic thinking disappears and one perceives things with a new consciousness, called pure consciousness. It is when I reach rock bottom, falling through every kind of thinking to the sheer emptiness of my being, that the Truth reveals itself. As St. Paul wrote about Jesus:

> His state was divine,
>     yet he did not cling to his equality with God,
> but emptied himself
>     to assume the condition of a slave,
>     and became as men are.
> And being as all men are
>     he was humbler yet,
>     even to accepting death,
>     and death on a cross.
> But God raised him high,
>     and gave him the name
>     which is above all other names,

> so that all beings
>> in the heavens, on earth and in the underworld,
>> should bend the knee
>> at the name of Jesus,
> and that every tongue should acclaim
>> Jesus Christ as Lord
>> to the glory of God the Father. (Phil. 2:6–11)

With this new consciousness one sees all things as "one"; one realizes as a delightful reality the saying of St. Paul:

> All things belong to you,
> you belong to Christ,
> and Christ belongs to God. (1 Cor. 3:22–23)

God is not "out there" while we are "here." We are in God and God is in us. This happened to me. After a long period of hard abiding on this koan of the "empty hand," one day in the winter of 1972, about two o'clock in the morning, I was on my way from the washroom to my cell in the dormitory. As I walked down the hall, suddenly there seemed to be something sweeping into me and elating my whole being, producing a sensation I had never experienced before, even after many years as a monk. I felt as if I were being carried above the ground, although I was fully alert and knew that my two feet were on the floor. I *was* the man riding the water buffalo. A whole realm of undifferentiated consciousness overwhelmed me. I felt a complete break from my past manner of thinking and feeling. Nothing remained of myself. An ineffable sense of release, well-being, and clarity of mind inundated me.

This state of being placed me in an exalted mood, which culminated two days later when I woke from sleep at three o'clock in the morning. Suddenly I was given to realize the truth of St. Paul's statement, "The risen body of Christ has become the life-giving Spirit" (1 Cor. 15:44). Christ pervaded and continues to pervade my whole being. My arms are "empty" but full of the intimate love of Jesus. Since then, my faith in the mystery of the risen body of Christ has become an experiential reality: I saw, or rather, I should say, I *realized* it as clearly as an apple in the palm of my hand. The result of my life in union with Jesus fills me with an extraordinary transparency and delight, an experience that springs up and erupts in the deepest recesses of my being. This causes a flaming passion in my soul fully equal in intensity to the intimate encounter of a man and a woman. A joy goes to the very depth of my existence and calls into play all the powers of my being—physical, psychological, intellectual, and spiritual.

Having gone through all this and having shared these events, I can now give a descriptive definition of contemplative experience for Christians. It is "an experiential realization of our intimate union with God in Christ Jesus."

### CHAPTER 2

# Intimate Union
# as Seen in
# Judeo-Christian Scriptures

IN THE HEBREW SCRIPTURES, a theme dear to the prophets is God's passionate love for Israel and Israel's joy in returning that love to its God. As a husband is to his wife, so Yahweh is to his people. The Hebrew prophets did not find this identification too bold or too daring. Isaiah wrote:

> Your Maker is your husband. (54:5)

and:

> As the Bridegroom rejoices over the Bride,
> so shall your God rejoice over you. (62:5)

Ezekiel also was emphatic. He used allegorical language to castigate Israel, the "faithless wife" of Yahweh. His imagery in chapter 16, a blow-by-blow account of harlotry, is undoubtedly offensive to our present-day tastes but still provides a lot to reflect on. Though not repudiated by God, Israel has been so unfaithful that her return and reconciliation would be a miracle of grace.

In Jeremiah's writings, God bitterly complains against Israel:

> If a man divorces his wife
> and she leaves him
> to marry someone else,
> may she still go back to him?

> Has not that piece of land
> been totally polluted?
> And you, who have prostituted yourself
>     with so many lovers,
> you would come back to me?
>         It is Yahweh who speaks. (Jer. 3:1–2)

Using the same analogy, Hosea presses the argument to its conclusion:

> Then she will say: "I will go back to my first husband.
> I was happier then than I am today." (Hos. 2:7)

Like Gomer, Hosea's faithless wife, Israel pursues happiness but misses out on it, seeks love from others but never finds it. She never found what she went after. She sought happiness away from Yahweh but found sorrow, sought fulfillment but found frustration, looked for satisfaction but found remorse. In pursuing her lovers and turning her energies toward relationships that seemed real but proved vain—that is, with false gods and hedonistic living—Israel was really expressing her hunger for God's love. In order to listen to the words of God's love, according to Hosea, Israel must enter into the embrace of silence and solitude where God draws near:

> That is why I am going to lure her
> and lead her into the wilderness
> and speak to her heart tenderly. . . .
> I will betroth you to myself forever
> Betroth you with integrity and justice
> With tenderness and love. (Hos. 2:16, 21)

The wilderness seems an unlikely place to find strength and comfort. When one wishes to speak words of comfort to someone, one normally does not choose such desolate surroundings. Yet God often does exactly this. His most profound revelations have come

in the most unlikely places. The deepest insights in the Hebrew
Scriptures do not come from the era of King Solomon, when
Israel was prosperous and flourishing; rather, they come out of
the wilderness of Sinai amid privation and great insecurity, or
during the time of exile and captivity. Even as the stars shine
most brightly when the night is darkest, so God seems to speak
the most burning words to the heart when everything seems to
be dark and dismal.

In order to express the resumption of the loving relationship
between Israel and her Husband Yahweh, Jeremiah wrote:

> Yahweh is creating something new on earth:
> the woman sets out to find her Husband again.
>
> (Jer. 31:32)

Faced with this passage, a biblical scholar might be at a loss to
educe its proper meaning, but the humble contemplative under-
stands it intuitively. He or she will read the text as referring to the
intimate loving relationship between Israel and Yahweh, her husband, which will culminate in the mystery of the virginal marriage
of Christ to his church. For the Christian contemplative, these
two concepts are always linked and illuminate one another. The
intimate union of husband and wife in marriage is a symbol of
Christ's union with his church. Paul makes this point explicit in
his teaching in Ephesians 5:32, when he instructs husband and
wife to love one another as Christ loves the church and the
church loves Christ.

In a similar vein, in Revelation 19:7–9 John writes:

> The reign of the Lord our God Almighty has begun.
> Let us be glad and joyful and give praise to God,
> because this is the time for the marriage of the Lamb.
> His bride is ready,
> and she has been able to dress herself in dazzling
>   white linen,

> because her linen is made of the good deeds
>     of the saints. . . .
> Happy are those who are invited to the wedding
>     of the Lamb.

At the end of time, when the eternal reign of God has begun, Christ and his Bride, the church, are united as one, and the entire communion of saints joins in the marriage feast. It is a profound vision of the triumph of love—the most intimate and tender love that we human beings know. Concluding the book of Revelation —and in fact, the whole Bible—John extends this invitation to love even further: to each one of us, universally.

> The Spirit and the Bride say, "Come!"
> Let everyone who listens answer, "Come!"
> Then let all who are thirsty come.
> All who want it may have the water of life,
> and have it free. (Rev. 22:17)

### CHAPTER 3

# Erotic Love and Spiritual Union

I AM A MEMBER OF THE CHURCH, the Mystical Body of Christ, and thus of the personification of the church as the Bride of Christ, and my contemplative experience has been a living out of those aspects of intimate union that are expressed in Scripture as the "bridal" or the "ecclesial" union. Obviously, this image is not the exclusive property of women. Many male saints, such as Bernard of Clairvaux and John of the Cross, have, like the women mystics, lived it and have explained their vocation in its light.

Since my own contemplative experience so strongly reflects a bridal, or ecclesial, dimension, and since the relationship of humans with God is pictured in these same terms in Sacred Scripture and in the mysticism of both East and West, some clarification of this aspect might be helpful.

The "moments" of contemplative experience are the golden moments when we experience ourselves as deeply loved. We are loved to the marrow of our bones. Christ is truly our Father and Lord, but he is something more intimate and more mysterious than that—something inexplicable in human language. It is more like the love of the bridegroom and the bride, and there is no other response on the part of the bride except love and joy. The imagery of this "bridal relationship" comes to us straight from divine revelation as well as from human experience. The richest validation of its truth is the divinely inspired Song of Songs in the Bible.

When determining which books to include in the Bible, some Jewish scholars apparently argued that the Song of Songs should not be included; its vivid description of human erotic love, in their view, made the book anything but holy text. However, Rabbi Joseph ben Akiva, a scholar and supporter of the unsuccessful Second Judean Revolt against the Romans (133–135 C.E.), said:

> All the writings in the Bible are holy,
> but the Song of Songs is the Holy of Holies.[1]

Without mincing words, the rabbi explains:

> The love between a man and a woman and the sexual intimacy to which that love leads is eminently worthy of God and eminently worthy to be the subject of a book of the Scripture. God forbid that there should ever have been a dispute in Israel about whether the Canticle is holy! The entire history of the world from its beginning to this very day does not outshine the day on which this book was given to Israel. All Scriptures, indeed, are holy and sacred to the hands that touch them. But the Canticle [the Song of Songs] is the Holy of Holies.[2]

The Song of Songs has been called a gem of literature; in our Judeo-Christian mystical tradition it has become an authoritative treasury of words and images for the contemplative experience. Here is a sampling:

> I am my Beloved's
> And my Beloved is mine. . . .
> Come, let us go into the field,
> let us stay in the village.
> Let us go early to the vineyards
> to behold whether the vine blossoms have budded,

> whether the pomegranates are in flower.
> There I will give you my love. (Song of Songs 7:12–13)

In both East and West the Song of Songs is revered for profundity and boldness. While many modern readers are content to see it simply as a celebration of the joys of sensual love, the Christian mystical tradition has always pushed beyond this level to emphasize its allegorical and transformative aspects. Read rightly—that is, from a contemplative awareness—it presents itself as a profound teaching on the transformation of human erotic and sexual desire to undergird a deeper union with God.

### Erotic and Sexual Caring

It is important to recognize at the outset that there are fundamental differences between the way traditional Christian mystics viewed love and desire and how this force is often seen in the contemporary world. As Bernard McGinn observes in *The Foundations of Mysticism:* "Some modern psychologists argued that the introduction of erotic language about God into a mystical account cannot be more than a disguise and an attempt at sublimating hidden sexual urges."[3] The mystics themselves, however, would hardly see it that way! An explanation of the term *eros* and the use of the erotic model to describe love of God are in order.

The Greek term *eros* means love, love for beautiful things. In Plato's *Symposium* Socrates recounts Diotima's instruction on "love matters." According to Diotima, love connects the heavenly and earthly realms. The lover's love for beautiful things is essentially a desire for the happiness that comes from the permanent possession of the Beautiful, which is identical with the Good. Such possession cannot be perfect if it comes to an end, and therefore love involves a longing for immortality. Diotima insists:

The ultimate goal of love is not for mere possession, but for generous begetting. It is of engendering and begetting upon the beautiful. Begetting according to the body is not condemned, but the begetting according to the soul which brings forth virtues is praised as more noble.[4]

In *The Four Loves* C. S. Lewis writes:

Eros is that state which we call "being in love," or if you prefer, that kind of love which lovers are "in." Sexual experience can occur without Eros, without being "in love," and that Eros includes other things beside sexual activity.... Without Eros, sexual desire, like every other desire, is a fact about ourselves. Within Eros it is rather about the Beloved. It becomes almost a mode of perception, entirely a mode of expression. It feels objectively, something outside of us, in the real world. That is why Eros, though the king of pleasures, always (at his height) has the air of regarding pleasure as a by-product.[5]

In *Love and Will* Rollo May, an eminent American psychologist, relates an early Greek myth about Eros:

Eros created life on Earth. When the world was barren and lifeless, it was Eros who "seized his life-giving arrows and pierced the cold bosom of the Earth," and "immediately the brown surface was covered with luxuriant verdure...." Eros then breathed into the nostrils of the clay forms of man and woman and gave them the "spirit of life." Ever since, eros has been distinguished by the function of giving the spirit of life, in contrast to the function of sex as the release of tension.

Rollo May clearly distinguished eros from sex:

Sex can be defined fairly adequately in physiological terms as consisting of the building up of bodily tensions and their release. Eros, in contrast, is the experiencing of the personal intentions and meaning of the act. Whereas sex is a rhythm of stimulus and response, eros is a state of being. The pleasure in sex is described by Freud and others as the reduction of tension; in eros, on the contrary, we wish not to be released from the excitement but rather to hang on to it, to bask in it, and even to increase it. The end toward which sex points is gratification and relaxation, whereas eros is a desiring, longing, a forever reaching out, seeking to expand.[6]

In *Eros and Allegory: Medieval Exegesis on the Song of Songs*, Denys Turner explains why the erotic model for the love of God was so appealing to the monastic commentators of the Song of Songs:

> The reason why the erotic model of the love of God so appealed to the monastic commentators of the middle ages—and the vast majority of these commentators were monks—had to do with very fundamental preoccupations of the monastic theologian, and these, in turn, were intimately connected with the monks' pre-conception of their *Sitz im Leben*. I shall not anticipate here the account I give later of what these preoccupations and perceptions were; suffice to say that they are rooted in the monks' theological eschatology, in their sense that their life of partial withdrawal from the world situated them at a point of intersection between this world and the next, between time and eternity, between light and dark, between anticipation and fulfillment. This meant that the concept of love as a *yearning*—or, in Greek, "*eros*"—exactly expressed what they wanted by way of a language of love.[7]

Origen, the third-century Christian mystic and church father, stands at the head of those Christian mystics who have argued that given the inadequacy of language to convey the ineffability of mystical experience, erotic language is the most appropriate way of using speech to surpass itself. He agreed with Plato and the other sages that

> although eros is usually experienced in relation to a human lover, it is in reality a heavenly force. The power of love is none other

than that which leads the soul from earth to the lofty heights of heaven, and the highest beatitude can only be attained under the stimulus of love's desire.[8]

According to Origen, the Song of Songs is the central textbook for "epoptics," that is, the place where Scripture reveals the highest of its messages about the love of the descending Christ for the fallen soul. It is in the interpretation of the erotic language of the Song that the deepest inscription of the mystical message takes place.[9]

Origen further observes: "I do not think one could be blamed if one called God Passionate Love (*eros/amor*), just as John calls him Charity (*agapē/caritas*)."[10]

### *The Allegorical Mode*

For more than a thousand years of Christian tradition, allegory was the major way of interpreting Scripture. Speaking of the function of allegory in interpreting Scripture, St. Gregory the Great, pope and sixth-century mystic, in his *Exposition on the Song of Songs* writes:

Allegories supply the soul separated far from God with a kind of mechanism by which it is raised to God. By means of dark sayings in whose words a person can understand something of his own, he can understand what is not his to understand, and by earthly words he can be raised above the earth. Therefore, through means which are not alien to our way of understanding, that which is beyond our understanding can be known. By that which we do know—out of such are allegories made—divine meanings are clothed and through our understanding of external speech we are brought to an inner understanding. Thus it is that in this book, called *The Song of Songs*, we find the words of a bodily love: so that the soul, its numbness caressed into warmth by familiar words, through the words of a lower love is excited to a higher.

For in this book are described kisses, breasts, cheeks, limbs; and this holy language is not to be held in ridicule because of these words. Rather we are provoked to reflect on the mercy of God; for by his naming of the parts of the body by which he calls us to love we must be made aware of how wonderfully and mercifully he works in us; for he goes so far as to use the language of our shameful loves in order to set our heart on fire with holy love. Thus in humbling himself by the manner of his speech he raises us in understanding; we learn, from the words of this lower love, with what intensity we must burn with love of God.[11]

It would be easy to pile up quotations from the early fathers of the church regarding the erotic and allegorical interpretation of the Song of Songs. One very interesting variation on the usual bridegroom/bride theme comes from St. Augustine of Hippo, (b. 354), one of the most profound and influential voices of the Christian mystical tradition. As Bernard McGinn acutely observes in *The Foundations of Mysticism:*

Augustine the young convert, who had so recently and wrenchingly abandoned an active sex life, did describe something of an erotic relationship to God, but through a rather unusual metaphor, one which is couched not in terms of the symbolism of the female Bride of the Song and her love for Christ, but in that of the relation of the male lover to the feminine figure of divine Wisdom (Proverbs 6 and 8).[12]

While the metaphor is different, the essential erotic components remain the same: burning zeal and a total commitment to the beloved. In his *Soliloquies* (winter 386) Augustine has Reason [Holy Wisdom] put into words the essential requirements for this path:

[Reason:] Now, we are trying to discover what kind of a lover of Wisdom you are: that Wisdom which you desire to behold and to possess with purest gaze and embrace, with no veil between and, as it were, naked, such as Wisdom allows to very few and these the most chosen of its lovers. If you were inflamed with the love of some beautiful woman, would she not rightly refuse to give herself to you if she discovered that you loved anything but herself? And will the purest beauty of Wisdom reveal itself to you unless you burn for it alone?[13]

McGinn further observes that Augustine does not abandon this theme of the lover of Wisdom—it occurs several times in the early homilies on the Psalms. A survey of these texts indicates that what he found most useful in this type of erotic language was the contrast between human eros, in which the male lover wishes to keep the sight and enjoyment of the beautiful female for himself, and the beauty of unclothed divine Wisdom, who offers herself freely and is shared by all her lovers without jealousy.[14]

So much for the early church fathers. For several more statements in the same vein by many patristic and medieval commentators, see Denys Turner's *Eros and Allegory*. Turner himself furnishes a fitting conclusion for this chapter from those pages:

The language of the love of God in the Western Christian tradition is notably erotic. This is unmistakably, even notoriously true of the Spanish Carmelites of the sixteenth century, John of the Cross and Teresa of Avila, who have so marked Catholic thought, language and experience in the subsequent three centuries. The Western Christian has traditionally been a female soul in love with her Bridegroom. She has fallen in love with him (Song 2:16). That love afflicts, soothes, thrills with the anticipation of consummation (Song 8:3). . . . The story of the soul is a love story. Here is no longer a language of a royal race, or even of people made one by *agapē*. These are the ones distinctly of eros, a language of heterosexual love.[15]

## PART TWO

# A Holy Desire

### CHAPTER 4

# Moving toward a Holy Desire

EROS IN GREEK MEANS PASSIONATE LOVE, passionate desire or yearning. As we learned from Rollo May earlier, sex and eros are different: sex is "the building up of bodily tensions and their release," whereas eros is "a state of being." Sexual pleasure is found in the release of tensions; in eros, on the contrary, one wishes "not to be released from the excitement but rather to hang on to it, to bask in it."[1]

This tendency in eros causes a great danger. In *The Four Loves,* C. S. Lewis warns us about this danger. Personifying eros, he writes:

> It is in the grandeur of Eros that the seeds of danger are concealed. He has spoken like a god. His total commitment, his restless disregard of happiness, his transcendence of self-regard, sound like a message from the eternal world. And yet it cannot, just as it stands, be the voice of God Himself; for Eros speaking with that very grandeur, and displaying that very transcendence of self may urge to evil as well as to good. We must not give unconditional obedience to the voice of Eros when he speaks most like a god. Neither must we ignore or attempt to deny the godlike quality. This love is really and fully like Love Himself. In it there is a real nearness to God. His total commitments are a paradigm or example built into our nature, of the love we ought to exercise toward God and men.[2]

Origen believed that human eros has its source above and has been implanted in us by God, but the eros gone astray in us must be transformed back to its transcendent starting place. This transformation is governed primarily by a redirection of the object of desire, or of eros. He insisted that human eros can only be transformed by turning it away from the inferior material and human object to which it has become directed in its fallen state. Hence, any form of erotic practice, especially sexual love, is irrelevant for the transformative process.[3]

In 2 Corinthians 4:16 Paul speaks of the outer and the inner person, that is, the person of flesh and the person of spirit: "Though the outer man may be falling into decay, the inner man is renewed day by day." Following Paul's distinction, Origen spoke of the two creations. The inner person, or first creation, is the one created in the image and likeness of God (see Gen. 1:26); the outer, or second creation, is "formed from the slime of the earth" (Gen. 2:7). The objects to which the outer person directs human eros—whether they be grossly materialistic things such as money, vainglory, or sexual pleasure, or even the higher goods of human arts and learning—are all transitory and unworthy of true eros. The only true goal of eros is the spiritual good of the first creation, the manifestation of Divine Eros.[4]

When asked how a spiritual seeker learns to read the inner text behind the erotic and longing language in the Song of Songs, Origen bridges the gap between the inner and the outer person, between heavenly and carnal love, by means of the *spiritual senses of the soul*. He developed this idea from Clement of Alexandria (150–220); it is one of the most important contributions to the history of Christian mysticism. Bernard McGinn summarizes:

According to the Alexandrian, "the divine scriptures make use of homonyms, that is to say, the use of identical terms for describing different things . . . so that you will find the names of the members of the body transferred to those of the soul; or rather, the faculties and powers of the soul are to be called its members." . . . Therefore, any bodily description contained in the Bible (and what book of Scripture contains more potent descriptions of body parts and bodily activities than the Song?) is actually a message about the inner person's relation to the Word because this person possesses "spiritual senses" analogous to the senses of taste and touch, hearing, smell, and sight by which the outer person relates to the material world [*De Principiis* 1.1.9]. Seeking the proper understanding of the erotic language of the Song is the exemplary exercise by which these higher and finer "senses" of the fallen, dormant intellect are awakened and resensitized by the spirit in order to be made capable of receiving the transcendental experience of the presence of the Word. Through these "organs of mystical knowledge," which Origen calls "a sensuality which has nothing sensual in it" [*Against Celsus* 1.48], the sharpness of sensual experience is brought back to its primordial intensity.[5]

According to St. John Climacus, a sixth-century mystical theologian, when we love God with the strength of eros, then eros is transformed into *agapē,* the spiritual love that comes from above. With telling psychological acuity he wrote:

I have seen impure souls, who threw themselves headlong into physical "*Eros*" to a frenzied degree. It was their very experience of that Eros that led them to interior conversion. They concentrated their *Eros* on the Lord. Rising above fear they tried to love God with insatiable desire. That is why when Christ spoke to the woman who had been a sinner he did not say that she had been afraid, but that she had loved much, and had easily been able to surmount love by love.[6]

St. Gregory of Nyssa (335–395), the great Cappadocian monastic legislator and anti-Arian bishop, in his *Homilies on the Song of Songs,* wrote:

Human understanding left to its own resource could neither discover nor absorb the Song's mystery. The most acute physical pleasure (I mean erotic passion) is used as a symbol in the exposition of this doctrine on love. It teaches us of the need for the soul to reach out to the divine nature's invisible beauty and to love it as the body is inclined to love what is akin to itself. The soul must transform passion into passionlessness so that when every corporeal affection has been quenched, our mind may seek with passion (erotically) for the spirit alone and be warmed by that fire which the Lord came to cast upon the earth.[7]

Eros, or yearning, or passionate love, is an authentic starting point for understanding and communing with the true nature of God. What is needed, and what mystical contemplative tradition is all about, is a way of transcending the usual sexual parameters of this love so that passionate yearning, when it lets go of its usual objects of gratification, becomes powerfully alive in intimate union with God in Christ Jesus. In the next few chapters I will attempt to offer my readers important "living food" for this transmutation, or transformation.

### CHAPTER 5

# The Eucharist

"**G**OD IS LOVE," SAID ST. JOHN, known in the Bible as "the disciple whom Jesus loved." The Eucharist, to me, is *the* manifestation, the personal overflowing of that love. Thus, when I unite myself with Jesus in the Eucharist, either through real holy communion or spiritual communion, I feel myself plunged deep into that love. In holy communion I hear the words of Jesus, "This is my Body given to you!" in a particularly vivid and physical way. I open the innermost of my being to receive Jesus, and with the same innermost of my being I say to Jesus, "This is my body given to you." This mutual giving and receiving gives me the satisfaction of my strongest yearning. I realize experientially that Jesus gives me his true body, his risen body, and not merely his will or something abstract.

When Our Lord declared, "The one who eats my flesh and drinks my blood remains in me and I in him," he was thinking not merely of a unity of will but of a unity of the flesh. Caryll Houselander's statement makes a lot a sense:

> On the night before He died Christ took bread into his hand, blessed and broke it, and gave it to His disciples, saying: "Take it and eat it; this is my Body!" In giving himself to the world, He deliberately chooses to emphasize the Body. Why? The body is, for us, the means by which we can give ourselves wholly. We say, "Go,

my thoughts are with you," or "My soul is with you." And we know that though something of ourselves is with the traveller, essentially we remain separate from him. We can give someone devoted care, unfailing kindness, and all our worldly possessions, but still we have kept ourselves. But when we give our body willingly to another as the means of deliberate donation, then our union with the other is complete. We surrender our intimacy, the secret of ourselves, with the giving of our body, and we cannot give it without our will, our thought, our minds and our souls. Christ surrenders the secret of Himself to each one of us when He gives us his Body. In Holy Communion this surrender of the secret of Himself goes on.[1]

This is the way Jesus gives himself to me, by giving me his Body. And when he says: "This is my Body given to you," I can in all truth say to him in return, "This is my body given to you." This mutual giving and receiving between Jesus and me gives both of us an ineffable repose. And this repose leads me to a full awareness of my human-divine wholeness.

The Eucharist is, as Jesus said, the life-giving bread, the real power of the resurrection communicated directly to our hearts and minds and bodies. Certainly it needs to be received in faith, and there needs to be an encounter within which the transmission of divine energy may take place. Thus, the real contact between Jesus and myself must be realized in order for the eucharistic fire and love to spread through my soul and body. The receiving of the consecrated bread and wine is the receiving of Christ "in the sacrament," that is, the receiving of Jesus through the sacramental signs. The receiving of the body and blood of Christ must lead us to the receiving of the real risen body of Jesus, the receiving that joins two flesh in one flesh. Jesus assures us that "the one who eats my flesh and drinks my blood lives in me and I live in that one" (John 6:56). This union with Christ— one flesh in two persons—is expressly nuptial and has been cele-

brated as such in our tradition in a symbolism that applies to the
church as a whole as well as to every soul that makes itself "ecclesial," or bridal, in its response to Christ. Three major symbols of
union with Christ in the Eucharist are the marriage at Cana (John
2:1–12), the marriage supper of the Lamb (Rev. 19:9), and the festive imagery of the Song of Songs. We see a good example of this
third type of symbolism in St. Gregory of Nyssa's commentary on
the Song of Songs:

> For those acquainted with the hidden meaning of the Scripture,
> the invitation to the mystery that was given to the apostles is identical with that of the Song of Songs: "Eat, O friends, and drink."
> In both cases, in fact, it is said, "Eat and drink deeply" . . . and the
> intoxication is Christ himself.
>
> Once the bridegroom has addressed her spouse, the Song offers
> the bride's companions the mystery of the Gospel saying: "Eat, my
> companions, and drink, be inebriated, my brethren" (5:1). To the
> person familiar with the Gospel's mystic words, there is no difference between this sentence and the words applied to the disciples'
> mystic initiation: in both cases it says "Eat and drink" (Matt
> 26:26–27). The bride's exhortation to her friends seems to have
> more weight than those in the Gospel. If anyone carefully examines both texts, he will find the Song's words to be in agreement
> with the Gospel, for the words addressed to the companions are
> brought to fruition in the Gospel. All inebriation makes the mind
> overcome with wine go into ecstasy.
>
> Therefore, what the Song enjoins becomes reality by that divine
> food and drink of the Gospel; as then and always, this food and
> drink contains a constant change and ecstasy from a worse to a
> better condition.[2]

I myself have experienced this "intoxication of Christ" that St.
Gregory speaks of. In holy communion, the union of Jesus' body
and my body and soul are so intimately deep that it sometimes
makes me inebriated. "He anoints my head with oil," writes the

psalmist, "my cup is overflowing" (Ps. 23:5a). My inmost being is so full it makes me intoxicated. Again a strong faith and an intense love are needed for this intoxication to happen.

Holy communion reminds me also of St. Paul's words: "Every time you eat this bread and drink this cup, you proclaim his death until He comes in glory" (1 Cor. 11:26–27). When Jesus said, "This is my Body given for you," I realize that the bread I receive is his crucified body given for me, that in sharing this body I have also been given to share his passion and death. The crucified body of Christ gives me the strength to endure all the inconveniences of my daily life. Sometimes after receiving holy communion I have been tempted to say as Paul said to the Corinthians: "During my stay with you the only knowledge I claimed to have was about Jesus, and only about him as the crucified Christ" (1 Cor. 2:2).

I like to borrow from Hugh of St. Victor, an eleventh-century philosopher, theologian, and mystical writer, to describe in part what I experience almost every time I receive holy communion:

> It is truly the Beloved who visits you.
> Yes, but he comes invisible, hidden, and incomprehensible.
> He comes to touch you, not to be seen,
> He makes you taste of him, not to pour himself out
>   in you entirely.
> He comes to draw your affection, not to satisfy your desire.
> To bestow the first fruit of his love, not to communicate it
>   in its fullness.
> Behold in this the most certain pledge of your future
>   marriage,
> that you are destined to see him and to possess him entirely,
> because he already gives himself to you to taste
>   with what sweetness you know.
> Therefore in times of his absence you shall console yourself,
> and during his visit you shall renew your courage.[3]

In holy communion I do not "see" the risen body of Jesus. There is no need for me to see him. I do experience his deep intimate "touch." He does not pour himself out entirely to me, but he gives as much as my weak human being can bear. He does not communicate the fruit of his love in its fullness, but he comes to draw my affection and purify my desire. And this is always the high point of my contemplative experience, the moment of intimate union with Jesus.

# Suffering Love

THE LOVER IN THE SONG OF SONGS asks to be sustained with raisins and refreshed with apples because she is sick or wounded with love (Song 2:5). This sickness is caused by the intense longing of one separated from her beloved. The same sickness is equally applicable to an ordinary soul separated from Christ. This is why St. Paul said, "For me to live is Christ and to die is gain" (Phil. 1:21).

The language of love is infinitely more than words and phrases. Love expresses itself not so much in what it says as in what it is and does. In the Song of Songs the lovers speak of their love in exquisite language and glory in the intimacy of their union. Hence, the maiden is distraught when she is separated from her lover.

This intimate personal presence is likewise at the heart of the Christian view of love. In the Hebrew Scriptures, God communicates his love for Israel through the prophets, but in the Christian Scriptures God's word becomes flesh and dwells among us. Jesus' presence makes my heart full of joy, but his seeming absence at times makes my heart wounded. This is the law of love: joy and sorrow go together; they are like two faces of one coin. In the Letter to the Hebrews we are reminded:

> Let us not lose sight of Jesus, who leads us in our faith and brings it to perfection: for the sake of the joy which was still in the

future, he endured the cross, disregarding the shamefulness of it, and from now on has taken his place at the right of God's throne. (Heb. 12:2)

It has been said that if the Song of Songs has a climax, it is to be found in the familiar and often quoted line, "Love is strong as death. . . . Many waters cannot quench love, neither can flood drown it" (Song 8:6–7). Here is the Song's doxology to love: victorious, invincible, irresistible. The point is not merely that love is something beautiful and ineffable, but that it is a powerful force, as strong and irresistible as death itself, a consuming fire that withstands all efforts to quench its flame. Love's victory is set over against whatever threatens it—sufferings, both spiritual and physical, sickness, and the grave. This love has little to do with the sentimental platitudes of popular songwriters who proclaim that love is the sweetest thing in the world. The love of the maiden and the youth in the Song is a hard-won thing that emerges victorious and triumphant in spite of everything that would hinder and prevent it. St. Paul writes about the realities of true love as well:

> Loves bears all things, believes all things,
> Hopes all things, endures all things.
> Love never ends. . . .
> So faith, hope, love abide, these three;
> but the greatest of these is love. (1 Cor. 13:7–8, 13)

Commenting on Song 2:5, which says, "My heart is wounded with love," Origen reflected on the Word as the arrow or dart of the Father, whose love strikes or wounds the soul:

If there is anyone anywhere who has at some time burned with this faithful love of the Word of God; if there is anyone who has been pierced with the loveworthy spear of his knowledge, so that he yearns and longs for him by day and night, can speak of naught but him, would hear of naught but him, can think of nothing else, and is disposed to no desire nor longing nor yet hope, except for him alone; if such there be, that soul then says in truth, "I have been wounded by charity."[1]

It is this love that the Christian contemplative strives for. Such love, by its very willingness to suffer all things (including its own yearning) is purified of desire and becomes the expression of "the very fullness of God."

# Sacred Reading

JUDEO-CHRISTIAN RELIGION IS ESSENTIALLY the mystery of an encounter between human beings and God. In the beginning of the Bible, in Genesis, Adam and Eve are represented as standing in the presence of God and entering into dialogue with him:

> The man and his wife heard the sound of Yahweh God walking in the cool of the day, and they hid from Yahweh God among the trees of the garden. But Yahweh God called to the man: "Where are you?" (Gen. 3:9)

After the Fall, God spoke to us only through prophetic intermediaries. But in Jesus, Christians believe that God has once again entered into conversation with humankind directly and face to face:

> In many and various ways God spoke of old to our fathers by the prophets, but in these last days he has spoken to us by his son, whom he appointed the heir of all things, through whom also he created the world. (Heb. 1:1–2)

In Jesus Christ the Father has spoken the "last" word to us, not in the sense of "final" but in the sense of "ultimate." This ultimate and ever-renewing truth is revealed to us through Sacred Scripture.

We are not talking here simply about *intellectual* truth, a system of doctrine or beliefs. The church has always regarded the word of Scripture as a *living* word, another kind of "bread that comes down from heaven." The Second Vatican Council's Dogmatic Constitution on Divine Revelation (*Dei Verbum*) echoes this ancient understanding:

> Such is the force and power of the Word of God that it can serve the Church as her support and vigor and the children of the Church as strength for their faith, food for the soul, and a pure and lasting font of spiritual life. The Church forcefully and specifically exhorts all the Christian faithful to learn the surpassing knowledge of Jesus Christ, by frequent reading of the divine Scripture. Ignorance of the Scriptures is ignorance of Christ.[1]

Monastic tradition places great emphasis on what is called *lectio divina*, the devout or sacred reading of Scripture, that is, reading done in the presence of God and in a spirit of contemplation. In recent years, as the contemplative spirit has reemerged so strongly in the church, this practice has grown far beyond the walls of the monasteries and is being widely offered and taught as a way of opening ourselves more and more deeply to the power of this living Word. It is essential to assimilate the words in the silence of our heart. Only by doing so will we be able to integrate that Word of God with our life and to place our total being at the disposal of the Spirit.

### Guigo's Ladder

Guigo, a twelfth-century Carthusian monk, is credited with the division of sacred reading into a series of four steps: (1) reading, (2) meditation, (3) prayer, and (4) contemplation. This method is called "Guigo's Ladder." This four-step ladder was actually a refinement of the fourfold interpretation of Sacred Scripture, or "four senses of Scripture," commonly found in the patristic tradition. Each rung on the ladder corresponds to a different way of knowing the Word, a different level of spiritual understanding. These four senses of Scripture, usually identified as the literal, allegorical, moral, and anagogical (or mystical), are encapsulated in a medieval Latin formula as follows:

> *Litera gesta docet*
> *Quid credas allegoria*
> *Moralis quid agas*
> *Quo tendas anagogia.*

> The letter teaches what was done,
> Allegory, what you should believe,
> The moral sense, what you should do,
> The anagogic, where you are heading.

(1) The practice of sacred reading implies a careful attention to the literal sense of the text. (2) The effort of meditation that springs from this reading brings the use of reason and affectivity into play. We search and inquire into the text to see what it has so say about our own life and values; we look for the moral sense. (3) In *prayer*, we intuit that the text refers symbolically to the experience of God, and we pray for a deep, experiential realization of that experience—the allegorical sense, which is about deepening faith and deepening responsiveness. (4) Lastly, in contemplation, we experience a delightful foretaste of heavenly realities as perceived in the anagogical, or mystical, sense of the text.

## Reading

Reading is an attentive survey of the text in order to grasp the central idea. We begin to listen to the text by considering prayerfully: What is being said? What is the meaning of this sentence or paragraph? What is the truth being communicated? St. Augus-

tine—and in modern times Søren Kierkegaard, a Danish philosopher and theologian—said that Scripture is the love letter the
Father sends to his children. We read the text as we read a love
letter. This means that we read it forward and backward several
times; we read again to uncover the love hidden behind the letter
and between the lines. Perhaps a single word captures our attention. It is all right to linger on this word. We let the word speak
to us. We listen more and more to the word until we hear it as
fully as we can.

### Meditation

Meditation here does not mean primarily a discursive reasoning
but an "abiding," a "dwelling," upon the sacred text. To be sure,
intellectual inquiry is the primary tool used here as we probe for
the underlying meaning. But an affective personal attitude is very
important as we permit ourselves to hear the word as if it were
directly spoken to us as a message.

We believe that God *is* speaking to us personally through the
text, and we take God's word to heart. We invite God's word to
penetrate our mind and our heart and to awaken in the ground
of our being a response of surrender, of wonder, of repentance,
and of love. We assimilate the word and let it become a living part
of us. We let it reveal us to ourselves as if in a mirror. The light
of spiritual truth illumines weaknesses in us that we might not
wish to face. The word of God is sometimes a judgment on our
infidelities, and we can only pray that we have the courage and
humility to encounter the "Word" as David encountered Nathan
the prophet, who came bringing stern words of rebuke. We pray
for grace, mercy, and the fulfillment of our longings. In all these
ways we imitate the Blessed Virgin, who pondered the words of
God in her heart (Luke 2:19).

*Prayer*

In this stage our awareness shifts from the text to the Person—God, or Christ Our Lord. We converse with Jesus from the interior of our heart, in direct, personal conversation. The emotions of our heart pour forth from us with spontaneous freedom, with the urgency of the Phoenician woman asking Jesus for a crumb of bread that falls from the table for her dying child (Matt. 15:27) or the urgency of Bartimaeus asking Our Lord to cure his blindness (Mark 10:47). We pour out to God our feelings and desires, even asking to know him by direct experience. If his mercy permits and under the impulse of grace, our prayer of affection may pass into contemplation.

*Contemplation*

Here we desire simply to rest in the presence of God and remain with God. We know that God is near. We experience his nearness as a gentle, caring presence like the presence of a loving father, mother, or spouse. Now there is no need for words or thoughts. Our words and thoughts are absorbed into the loving awareness of silent presence. On a deep interior level we sense a calmness, a refreshment for our weariness, a satisfaction for our yearning, an anointing with the oil of gladness.

### Opening the Mind and Heart

We cannot do *lectio divina* from an ordinary frame of mind, full of urgency and rush. A special inner disposition is needed to allow the Word of Scripture to gradually unfold its deeper meaning. Here are some aspects of that disposition.

## Prayer

We need to pray for God's help when we approach the words of
the Scriptures. As Origen wrote to Gregory Thaumaturgus:

> For your part, then, apply all your zeal to the reading of Scripture,
> with faith and the good will that are pleasing to God. It is not
> enough for you to knock and seek. What is needed above all in
> order to obtain the understanding of divine matters is prayer.[2]

## Purity of Heart

On this aspect, John Cassian writes:

> To penetrate to the very heart and marrow of the heavenly words,
> and to contemplate their hidden and deep mysteries with the
> heart's gaze purified, can be acquired neither through human sci-
> ence nor through profane culture, but only by purity of soul,
> through the illumination of the Holy Spirit.[3]

## Upright Faith and Profound Humility

The most profound of the four senses of Scripture is called the
anagogical, or the mystical, sense. This refers to the power of
Scripture to lift up our hearts to spiritual realities and to lead us
deeper into prayer and contemplation. This mystical sense can be
grasped only through deep humility, as the fathers of the church
so often stressed. Alexander of Canterbury, a twelfth-century
Benedictine monk, uses the following analogy in commenting on
the words of the Song of Songs: "He has brought me into his
wine cellar" (Song 2:4):

> There are four casks in the wine cellar, each of which represents
> one of the four senses of the Bible. Anagogical (mystical) is
> defined as a sort of experience of the very sweet divine love; when

our soul recovers its forces in the ineffable sweetness of this love, it becomes united, in some way, to the sovereign divinity. Whoever has drunk from this anagogy will have tasted, be it ever so little, that divinity, and he will straightforward become inebriated by the marvelous sweetness of this drink.[4]

The wine cellar of the Scriptures is opened only by means of a double key: upright faith and profound humility. Someone might be able, like a thief, to break into the cellar by violence, and perhaps he might be able to lap up a few drops from the first three casks, because secular knowledge does have virtue of a sort. But in the case of the last of these casks, anagogy, there is no possible means for him to attain it. Even for the scholar, equipped with all the most perfect tools of research, the only solution for him, when it comes to anagogy, is the solution common to all the baptized faithful: like them, he too must scrutinize with humility the meaning of the Scripture as though he were standing at the door and knocking.

## Lingering in the Word

St. Bernard writes:

> The soul that thirsts after God gladly rests and lingers in God's inspired word, knowing that therein, without doubt, she shall find God for whose company she yearns.[5]

As for himself, he adds:

> I will search the treasure of spirit and life hidden in the profound depths of these inspired utterances. This is my inheritance, because I am a believer in Christ. Why should I not endeavor to find the wholesome and savory food of the spirits beneath the unprofitable letter, as the grain amongst the chaff, the meat in the shell, or the marrow in the bone?[6]

To express his eagerness and delight in reading Sacred Scripture, Bernard uses the same metaphor as St. Gregory the Great: "In the ocean of this sacred reading the lamb paddles, and the elephant swims." For this reason he added:

> Let no one be astonished or take it amiss if in examining the Scripture I give rein to my inquisitiveness as if I were in the wine-cellar of the spirit, since I know that life is found in this way and among such things my spirit draws strength.[7]

### *A Sense of Taste*

In order to explore the profound depths of sacred truth, we must develop what St. Bernard called a "sense of taste":

> Sacred Scripture, not content to flatter our eyes with the beauty of its literary cloth, wants to satiate us with the succulence of its profound meaning. It was written for us, not only to delight us with its external form, but also to feed the internal sense of taste as with the marrow of the wheat.[8]

### **Encountering the Living Jesus**

The purpose of sacred reading is not to gain information about God or Jesus but to encounter the living God, the living Jesus. All the words of the Scriptures—Hebrew and Christian alike—point to the person of Jesus. As recorded in the Gospel of Luke, on Easter day Jesus appeared to the two disciples on the road to Emmaus and opened the inner meaning of Scripture to them. Starting with Moses and going through all the prophets, he pointed out the scriptural passages that were about himself (Luke 24:27). In like manner, we too want to experience how the words of Scripture are about Jesus and to share the same response as the astonished disciples: "Did not our hearts burn within us as he spoke?"

(Luke 24:32). Therefore we do not stop at the mere words, either of the Hebrew Bible or the New Testament. We do not stop at biblical theology or commentaries. We go straight through the words to the very person of Jesus, who is the Word. We will have contemplative experience when we have encountered Jesus' words as "spirit and life" (John 6:63).

## The Place of the Heart

There is a place in us where God touches us, and where we ourselves are constantly in contact with God simply because at every instant God holds us in being. The place where this creative contact with God takes place is deep within us. If we can free ourselves from everyday preoccupations and bring the gaze of our spirit to bear on this point exclusively, we can meet God. The Bible gives this interior place its name: the heart.

St. Teresa of Avila, John of the Cross, the Rhineland mystics, and many others have spoken of this place as an abyss, or a well whose depth draws us like a magnet. They also speak of this place as the "apex of the soul," "the pinnacle of the spirit," and "the fine point of the soul." They invite us to enter this place where we all meet God, and which is therefore the most precious center of our being.

If the word of God is to bear fruit in us and become prayer, we must dwell in that place where we can hear and welcome the Word; we must return to the heart. Some monastic fathers designate the heart as "the place of God in us." Thus their advice to the novices is always the same: "Return to the heart."

# Reading Scripture as Reading a Zen Koan

AS I MENTIONED IN AN EARLIER CHAPTER, one of the influences that led me to my moment of contemplative breakthrough was a period of intense reflection on the Zen koan "Empty Hand":

> Empty hand, yet holding a hoe,
> Walking, yet riding a water buffalo.

It might be of some interest to you if I explain why I, a Christian monk, was engaged in Zen meditation.

The word *koan* (in Chinese, "*kung-an*") originally referred to a document relating to an official transaction. The term was adopted into Zen to mean a specific item demanding attention. The koan is a proposition for the mind beyond thought. It is usually prescribed by a Zen master and is of such a nature that it violates the postulates of logic. For example:

> You know the sound of two hands clapping,
> But what is the sound of one hand clapping?

When the disciple is presented with a koan to reflect on, it seems like a canvas consisting entirely of random brushstrokes, and he or she puzzles: What is the meaning of this? At first one is at a loss because the answer is not in the ordinary field of thought. The solution to the question must be gained by intuition, or by a sort of "mystical faculty." If one faces the koan with true faith, one tries, and keeps on trying, until suddenly a breakthrough occurs. The disciple "becomes one with the koan," so to speak, and "solves" the problem.

Here is my story. During my twenty years as novice master at St. Joseph's Abbey in the United States, I encountered hundreds of young Americans who were seeking to enter our monastery and who were searching for God. Nine out of ten of these young men would ask me, "Can you tell me something about Zen meditation? Having grown up in the East, you must know something about Zen." The fact was, however, that I came from a family that had been Christian for four hundred years, and from the earliest days of my childhood I had been taught only the Christian religion—not a single lesson on Zen Buddhism, let alone Zen meditation.

To their disappointment, I would tell them that it would be better not to involve themselves in a non-Christian practice, better to stay with the practice of prayer that they were familiar with, the practice taught to them by their Christian teachers.

But after a while, I began to realize that I had been too negative—in fact, ignorant—for after all, I did not really know anything about Zen meditation. So I began to study and to actually practice Zen meditation by myself. After one year of quite intensive study and faithful practice on my own, I received a breakthrough into the koan of the "empty hand" I mentioned above.

My inner perception into reality opened up. My ordinary consciousness was altered. I saw things differently: a glimpse into truth, into reality. As a matter of fact, I was gazing into the mystery of the Blessed Trinity as through a mirror; and through my faith and my love for Christ, the presence of Christ in the Eucharist and within my inmost being, became a reality.

After that happy event I joined a group of fellow monks who were being trained under the famous Japanese Zen master Joshu Sasaki Roshi. He had been coming to St. Joseph's Abbey at the invitation of the abbot, Fr. Thomas Keating, to teach the monks a Christian form of Zen meditation. During an eight-day Christian Zen retreat conducted by this same Roshi Sasaki, the Roshi gave us the following koan in the first meditation session:

> How do you realize God
> When you make the sign of the cross?

While listening to the Roshi give the koan, I thought, "That is easy!" I immediately remembered St. Paul's very forceful statement, "The cross is the power and the wisdom of God for those whom God has called" (1 Cor. 1:24).

I looked forward to my first encounter with the Roshi, intending to tell him my understanding of the koan. I started to "theologize" the koan according to St. Paul's teaching. But as soon as I opened my mouth, the Roshi rang his little bell, indicating that I must stop—"shut up!"—and get out. Since Zen is life and not a doctrine, I would have to demonstrate my grasp of the koan by a body–soul language and not by the words of theology.

I worked very hard on that "cross koan" eight hours a day for eight days! Each time I saw the Roshi and told him my progress, he rang me out. Then one day, instead of talking, I opened wide my arms like Jesus on the cross and experienced within myself the suffering, death, and resurrection of Jesus. It was the best way I could demonstrate to him how I had grasped the mystery of the cross. He was very pleased and indicated some satisfaction by giving me a new koan. As a rule, the Roshi will not give you a new koan unless you have "solved" the one at hand.

During that week-long retreat the Roshi told us time and again, "A monk who does not experience God when he makes the sign of the cross is not worth a penny; he is not a monk, let alone a Christian monk." He confided to us his own appreciation of the cross of Christ, saying:

> You may laugh at me when you see me, a Zen monk, making the sign of the cross. But when I make the sign of the cross, I feel like Jesus extending his arms to embrace the whole world, the whole universe, taking into himself all the sorrows and the joys of all living beings.

Later that week we gave him a Bible. Apparently he opened to St. John's Gospel at random and spent several hours reading. When he saw us the next day he told us there are many sayings in the Gospel that sound like the Zen koans. As an example, he chose Jesus' words to Nicodemus:

> The wind blows wherever it pleases—
> you hear its sound,
> but you cannot tell where it comes or where it is going.
> That is how it is with all who are born of the Spirit. (John 3:8)

I knew he had read that text of John and deeply grasped its meaning, because when I encountered him, he paraphrased these words of Jesus to Nicodemus and gave them to me as a koan. He asked:

> Jesus said, "You hear the wind,
> but you do not know where it comes from.
> Tell me, then: Where does the Spirit come from?"

I was terribly happy because I "solved" that koan very quickly. Since my faith tells me and in fact I experience that the Holy Spirit is within the depths of my being, I placed my hands upon my breast, demonstrating to the Roshi that the Spirit comes from within me. He gave me a happy smile!

The Roshi also read the account of our Lord's resurrection in one of the Gospels. He told us, "I like Christianity, because Christianity is the only religion that speaks about the resurrection." The term "resurrection" for us Christians is equivalent to the term "religious awakening" or "enlightenment" in non-Christian religions. In one of my early morning encounters with him he tested me:

> This is early morning.
> Jesus has risen from the dead!
> Show me your resurrection.

I "solved" this "resurrection koan" with no difficulty as I had the "Holy Spirit koan," because when we realize that the risen body of Christ has become the "life-giving Spirit" (1 Cor. 15:45), and that Jesus is dwelling within us, we will experience the resurrection of Jesus within us. We rise with Jesus in the inmost depths of our being, and our whole life itself is the resurrection.

There are many koans in the Bible. For example, at the Last Supper when Jesus instituted the Eucharist, he gave the bread to his disciple saying, "This is my Body!" This saying certainly goes beyond reason, beyond logic—and thus, it is a koan. In his *Christian Zen*, William Johnston writes:

> The Bible is one tremendous koan that makes the mind boggle and gasp in astonishment; and faith is the breakthrough into that deep realm of the soul which accepts paradox and mystery with humility.[1]

If we read the Sacred Scripture the way people read the Zen koans, we would certainly discover the mysteries—or "the spirit and life"—hidden in the words of the sacred texts.

## PART THREE

# Steps Leading to
# Contemplative Experience

# Five Steps to Contemplative Experience in the Song of Songs

IF YOU HAVE STAYED WITH ME THUS FAR, you may already have some ideas as to how to proceed toward contemplative experience. If you don't mind, please come along with me a bit further. My way to intimate union with Jesus—that is, to contemplative experience—is simple and humble: It is the intimacy of the lover with her beloved.

There are many passages in Sacred Scripture that can serve as signposts leading us gradually toward that intimacy. One text that has helped me greatly, for example, is Revelation 3:20:

> Look, I am standing at the door, knocking.
> If one of you hears me calling and opens the door,
> I will come in to share your meal
> Side by side with you.

To share one's meal means to share a table fellowship, to enter into intimacy. We notice here with what gentleness Our Lord enters into intimacy with us. He is standing at the door and knocking; he does not aggressively force our love. He will enter only if we voluntarily open our door to him. And once inside, he accepts our meal, our intimacy. This is the way; these are the steps we follow to enter intimacy with him, to have contemplative experience.

My own special favorite among these scriptural signposts is in the seventh chapter of the Song of Songs. As I have mentioned already, the Song of Songs is a "lamp unto the eyes" of all who are trying to follow a "bridal" or "ecclesial" path to contemplative experience through intimate union with Christ. In Song 7:11–13, five statements in the beautiful, veiled language of mystical symbolism speak to me of five steps, or five realizations, leading to the fullness of contemplative experience.

1. I am my Beloved's.
2. And my Beloved is mine.
3. Come, my Beloved, let us go to the field.
4. And see whether the grape blooms have opened.
5. There I will give you my love.

Before I share with you my personal practice, a few reminders are in order if our journey is to be effective. First, we are dealing here with a mystery of love to be contemplated and experienced, not with an academic theory to be deliberated. Like the sensible virgins of whom Our Lord speaks in the Gospel of Matthew, we must be alert and ready to respond to his call to the wedding banquet:

> Behold the bridegroom comes,
> go you out to meet him! (Matt. 25:6)

Second, let us recall that Jesus is God and God is love. As love, Jesus has an infinite desire to give himself in love to us. And we, being created in the image and likeness of God, are given an unlimited capacity to return ourselves in love to God.

Third, we need a strong intuitive faith. Our Lord assures us, "If you had faith the size of a mustard seed you could say to this mountain: 'Move from here to there,' and it would move. Nothing will be impossible to you" (Matt. 17:20). It is your faith that makes Jesus present to you, and it is with your love that Jesus embraces you.

Fourth, we need an interior vision, or visualization. This means that we need to let the words of God on which we meditate coincide with our inner seeing and feeling to create a strong interior experience of the situation. Take the words of step 1, for example: "I am my Beloved's," and then the words of step 2: "And my Beloved is mine." We need to meditate on—that is, to "dwell," to "abide in"—these words until they become a reality, a oneness within our inmost being, like a realized koan. The words should not just be carriers of an abstract idea. The word of God is spirit and life (John 6:63).

Finally, at every step it is important to call on the Holy Spirit. We pray that the Spirit burns our heart with its love and fills our mind with its wisdom. Wisdom is the capacity to taste God and the things of God.

Let us now proceed.

### *I Am My Beloved's*

The first step toward a contemplative experience, or toward an intimate union with Jesus, is to realize and to believe that we are loved by him and that we belong to him because he paid the price of his blood for us. We are made for Jesus and thus we long for him. We will not find rest until we rest in him. Longing here is not a desire to possess Jesus; rather it is an openness to him, a readiness to accept whatever he wants of us. We say as the Blessed Virgin did, "Behold the handmaid of the Lord, be it done to me according to your word."

Let the words of Scripture stir up your love for Jesus. Do not be afraid to have a desire, a longing, even a passionate love for Jesus. It is not you who call on him, but he, in his infinite mercy, who calls you to him. So, just say confidently and realize with all your heart, "I am my Beloved's."

### My Beloved Is Mine

The second step toward a contemplative experience is to realize and to believe that Jesus desires you; he wants you as his beloved. It is Jesus who first loves you and longs for you so that you are drawn to his intimate love. He takes the initiative. "I have come," he said, "to bring fire to earth, and how I wish it were blazing already!" (Luke 12:49).

You cannot take an aggressive step; it is for you to be totally open and receptive. In order to experience union, you must be passive while Jesus acts. St. John writes:

> This is love,
> Not that we loved God
> But that God loved us first. . . . (1 John 4:10)

It is through Jesus' prior love for us that he anticipates us, seeks us, and loves us before we seek him and love him. The power of Jesus' longing enables us to respond to his longing, and without this no one can come to him. This quality of longing and thirst comes from Jesus' everlasting kindness.

### Let Us Go to the Field

At this third step the mutual longing of Jesus and your own soul meet. There must be a place for this mutual longing to express itself. This place is like a garden in a field. There are two major aspects of this garden. It is, first, a place set apart, a place of solitude. The need for a private setting is easily understood. No one makes love in a public place. You are lured into seclusion, whether to the vineyard in the Song of Songs or to the desert wilderness, as in many other scriptural stories, in order for Jesus to speak to your heart (cf. Hos. 2:16).

When Our Lord wanted to reveal the secret of his love to the Samaritan woman, he went by himself alone to the field while all the disciples went to town. He sat at the well and waited for the woman to arrive. Scripture does not mention anybody else present at the well, only Jesus and the woman.

Early on Easter morning, Peter, John, and Mary Magdalene were all three at the tomb. Peter and John looked inside and outside the tomb and then left. Only Mary stayed behind. It was then that Jesus appeared to her and allowed her to recognize him as the risen Lord and to embrace him. Here is the mystery of privacy and the significance of solitude. Our Lord tells us, "When you pray, enter your room and shut the door" (Matt. 6:6). Behind the closed door your heart can express itself freely to Jesus.

Second, this garden is *yourself.* The Beloved of the Song says, "A garden locked is my sister, my bride, a spring, a fountain sealed" (Song 4:12). This means that you are exclusively Jesus'. Jesus wants you as his closed garden, his sealed fountain, alone to himself. Scripture says: "Yahweh your God is a consuming fire, a jealous God" (Deut. 4:24). God's jealousy is the extravagance of his love. St. Paul writes to the Corinthians, "You see, the jealousy that I feel for you is God's jealousy: I arranged for you to marry Christ so that I might give you away as a chaste virgin to this one husband" (2 Cor. 11:2). Jesus so loves you that he acts as though there is only you and he in the whole wide world.

At this step, when you realize the intensity of Jesus' longing for you and yours for him, you should begin to feel, as it were, a certain "touch," a certain "livingness" at the depths of your being, although you do not understand it. You can in all truth and spirit say, "I am my Beloved's, and he is mine!"

### *We Will See*
### *Whether the Grape Blooms Have Opened*

The "grape blooms" stand for you, for your love (Song 7:13). At this stage Jesus' desire for you reaches its zenith, and your longing for him attains its utter intensity. It is like the bow at its extreme tension, ready to act; what remains to be done is to release the arrow. Now, you are fully prepared for the last stage.

### *There I Will Give You My Love*

The moment Jesus and you give love to each other is a moment of unity, of consummation. Here, the state of intimate union, or contemplative experience, is achieved. The mutual repose between Jesus and you leads you to experience in full awareness your human–divine wholeness.

These are the signposts that have led me to my own contemplative experience. I hope they will lead you in the same way to yours. Remember that intimate union with Jesus is a mystery to be contemplated and experienced, not an academic theory to be discussed. It is faith that makes Jesus present to you, and love within which he embraces you.

# Contemplative Experience according to St. Bernard and Master Tozan Ryokai

I T PROBABLY SEEMS NATURAL that in my reading and meditation on the Word of God, I have been greatly inspired by the
mystical writings of St. Bernard of Clairvaux. But I have also
found very helpful the teachings of a ninth-century Zen master
named Tozan Ryokai. In this chapter I wish to set side by side the
insights of these two masters to see how they can help to awaken
in us the contemplative experience. In particular, I hope to use
their teachings to explain more fully the five steps that I introduced in the last chapter.

### St. Bernard of Clairvaux
### (1090–1153)

I have already spoken a good deal about St. Bernard, but perhaps
a more formal introduction would be helpful. Bernard of Clairvaux was born in 1090 at the castle of Fontaine-les-Dijon in France.
From his youth he demonstrated an amazing combination of tem-
perament and grace in many roles: poet, lover of nature, artist,
musician, thinker, biblical exegete, mystical theologian, writer,
and spiritual master. He is one of the first great spiritual fathers
of the Cistercian monastic order, of which I am a member. Thus,
he is my own spiritual father.

One of the great lights of the Middle Ages, Bernard left us a large body of writings. His best known works are his letters and his homilies; his most influential writings are a group of eighty-six conferences on the Song of Songs. Nowhere else are his profound spiritual insight and experience of God manifested with such depth, vitality, and spontaneity.

These conferences, given to his own monks, were the fruit of his mature years. His commentary on the Song of Songs is a magnificent treatise on the union of the Incarnate Word with the church, which is the same as the mystical union of the soul with the Word. Here we have Bernard's penetrating insight into the mystery of Christ and the mystery of the church.

Bernard's stature as a spiritual master has been immortalized in Dante's famous poem *The Divine Comedy*. During his journey from hell to paradise, Dante was given three guides: Virgil, Beatrice (his beloved), and Bernard. Virgil guided Dante, as it were, through the "purgative way," Beatrice through the "illuminative way," and Bernard through the "unitive," or "contemplative," way.

Surprisingly, although *The Divine Comedy* is a great love story, Beatrice is not Dante's ultimate guide. Beatrice's illuminative way is intellectual but not yet "sapiential"; nor is it a way of the "heart." It is up to Bernard to take over from Beatrice and guide Dante to the fullness of his own heart. On this point Etienne Gilson makes a very telling comment. Reflecting on a statement by Thomas Aquinas—"the greater one's love, the more perfectly one will see God, and the more blessed will one be" (*Summa Theologiae* 1, 12, 6 resp.)—Gilson writes:

> In the mind of anyone who understands this [Aquinas's statement] the role of St. Bernard in the *Divine Comedy* assumes an intelligible aspect and at the same time that of Beatrice appears in its

true light. The outcome of the Sacred Poem is nothing else than the union of the soul with God, the image of the beatific vision. If Beatrice were the light of glory, the *Divine Comedy* would conclude with a look from her eyes and a smile from her lips. But Beatrice retires and appoints in her place this man whom love has transfigured into the image of Christ—Bernard of Clairvaux.[1]

Like many eastern and western mystics, Bernard frequently presents "itineraries" of the soul's progress. For example, in *The Steps of Humility and Pride* he distinguishes twelve degrees of humility, the necessary ascetical preparation for the subsequent progress to mystical union. In Sermon 18 on the Song of Songs he mentions seven progressive stages that culminate in the fullness of love. In Sermon 85 he summarizes seven ascending reasons why the soul seeks the Word, and in Sermon 7 he speaks of the fourfold (also ascending) modes of love.

### Tozan Ryokai (807–869)

Tozan Ryokai—in Chinese, Tung-Shan Liang-chieh—was one of the founders of the Soto Zen sect in China. Two schools of Zen arose in China, the Soto and the Rinzai. In the former, the use of the koan was less important, and the greater emphasis was placed on the gentle method of sitting in quiet meditation. In the Rinzai school, both meditation and the koan were considered of equal importance.

The Soto Zen sect's teaching was taken to Japan by Dogen in 1227, where it flourished. The Soto sect now has more than fifteen thousand temples in Japan. I had the joy of visiting many of these magnificent temples and made a one-week retreat in one of them in Kyoto in 1983.

Training in the Soto school follows a system of five stages of meditation called the "five relations," devised by Tozan Ryokai, leading to full enlightenment. These five relations work with "paired opposites," of which the following are a few examples:

| | |
|---|---|
| Absolute | Relative |
| Infinite | Finite |
| Universal | Particular |
| One | Many |
| Unmanifested | Manifested |
| Eternal | Temporal |
| Permanent | Transient |
| Yang | Yin |
| Male | Female |
| Activity | Rest |
| Dynamic | Passive |
| Host | Guest |
| Real | Apparent |

A Christian might add:

| | |
|---|---|
| Yahweh | Israel |
| Christ | The Church |

These pairs are opposing yet cooperating aspects of one Reality. In order to experience that one Reality, one must go beyond the sway of the opposites to the totality that embraces them both.

Using the pair Host–Guest, Tozan Ryokai sets forth the five steps[2] (or five relations) through which the disciple must pass on the way to experiencing that one Reality. These five steps are as follows:

1. Guest in Host
2. Host in Guest
3. Resurgence of Host
4. Mutual Interpenetration
5. Unity Attained

Host stands for the great spiritual Reality, the principle of life, truth, and action. We Christians call it God. In contrast with it is Guest, the dependent, the soul, the visitor who must be received.

### East–West Conflict, or Harmony?

As I present Bernard's steps leading to contemplative experience alongside those of Master Tozan Ryokai, I am following the gradual development of Bernard's own contemplative experience rather than his specific models. Whenever one is considering the teaching and experience of St. Bernard, it is important to bear in mind that Bernard constantly insisted on the necessity of the personal experience of his listeners as the only way to understand his message. He began his comment on the personal meaning of the Song of Songs, "Today we read in the book of experience." Bernard's observations are also true for us: "In matters of this kind, understanding can follow only where experience leads."

The value of exploring what Master Tozan and St. Bernard have articulated lies in the heightened awareness of our own consciousness and in an intensified appreciation of our own values, for unless their experiences are also essentially ours, the beauty of their wisdom will have no appeal.

### CHAPTER II

# Step One: Guest in Host Experience

IN THE CHAPTERS THAT FOLLOW I HOPE to develop more fully the teaching and the experiences of these two masters, St. Bernard and Master Tozan Ryokai, concerning the five steps leading to contemplative experience. My hope is that a clear understanding of the teaching will guide you to fruitful practice.

The first step leading to the contemplative experience is the realization that the "Guest is in the Host," or that we are in God. This first step is an important one. We all know with an abstract knowledge that we have a soul, but how often, if ever, are we directly aware of that soul? In daily living, most of us are hardly aware that we truly live in God and that God is truly in us. Tozan describes the situation in the following verse:

> In the third watch of the night
> Before the moon appears.
> No wonder when we meet
> There is no recognition!
> Still cherished in my heart
> Is the beauty of earlier days.[1]

The reason for our unawareness of God being within us—in Tozan's words, "No wonder when we meet, there is no recognition"—is that the state of our inner perception of God is too dormant. Our knowledge of God is only "logical," slim, and vague. There is no warmth, no personal contact. This is the result of many layers of smoke and clouds that cover our inner eyes. In the confusion of greed and fear and other attachments (such as sentimentality and nostalgia for "the beauty of earlier days") we lose even the tracks of God's presence here and now.

For reasons that will become clear later, the modern Zen teacher D. T. Suzuki depicts this situation as a straight line, headed resolutely in a single direction.[2]

A ⟶ B

If in this single-minded purposefulness we should happen to pass by the one who might one day become our husband or wife, we would probably not even notice—particularly if the other one were in a similar mental state! Each one minds his/her own business; all the possibilities are there, but there is no spark of recognition; no warmth.

In order to dissipate the mental haze that clouds our perception, Master Tozan devised his first step, which is like a riddle, a koan, in that it is not logical. It says: "Guest in Host." You ask, "How in the world can one be in another?" (By asking this question you have imitated Nicodemus, who asked Our Lord, "How can a man enter his mother's womb a second time and be born again?" [John 3:4].) But after a period of intensive meditation on the "riddle," your effort begins to bear fruit. The inner candle is lighted and darkness is dispelled; you begin to have a gradual but *actual* experience of God's presence as a Host, here in the present moment.

We now look at St. Bernard for a parallel to this first step. In Sermon 14 on the Song of Songs Bernard laments this "coldness of heart," as he calls it, while yet dimly recognizing that something deeper is leading him on:

I am not ashamed to admit that very often, I myself, especially in the early days of my conversion, experienced coldness of heart while deep in my being I sought him whom I longed to love. I could not yet love him since I had not really found him. At best, my love was less than it should have been, and for that very reason I sought to increase it, for I would not have sought him had I not already loved him in some degree. I sought him therefore, in order that in him my numbed and languid spirit might find warmth and repose, for nowhere could I find a friend to help me, whose love would thaw the wintry cold that chilled my inward being, and bring back again the feeling of springlike bliss and spiritual delight.[3]

A story has been told that a baby fish one day came to its mother fish and asked:

"Mom, what is the ocean?"

With a gentle smile the mother fish answered, "My child, from the time you were hatched from the egg, you were living in the ocean. Ocean is all around you. You are living in it; you are playing in it all the time. If there were no ocean, there would be not one of us fish alive."

The answer satisfied the baby fish. She was happy and content to know that the ocean had been all around her all the time. The same is true for us. How happy we will all be when we experience that we are in God at all times!

To live a constant prayer, to lead a contemplative life, is nothing more than to live in the actual presence of God—moment by moment. Every one of us, indeed, by the very fact that we exist, is already in the presence of God, is already within God. To live in the presence of God should be as natural for us as to breathe the air that surrounds us, or to swim in the ocean like the baby fish.

### CHAPTER 12

# Step Two:
# Host in Guest

THE SECOND STEP LEADING to contemplative experience—
that is, to intimate union with God—is called "Host in Guest."
This second step guides us to the realization that God is already
in us. What is needed is an awareness of God's presence within
the depths of our being. Speaking to the Colossians about the
mystery that God is revealing to the Gentiles, St. Paul assures
them that the mystery he is talking about is "Christ in you, the
hope of glory" (Col. 1:27).

Exegetically, the preposition *in* used here means a close union
of Christ and the soul, an inclusion or incorporation connoting a
symbiosis, or a living together. Thus, it is important for us to
come to know this mystery of "Christ dwelling in us" as a reality.
Here are two stories that convey a sense of this realization:

> Some years ago a poor old man and his wife lived in a shack on
> the Oklahoma plains. One morning an engineer came up the path
> and asked if he could drill a test hole for oil under their kitchen
> floor. He found a gusher, tapped the oil out by the hundreds of
> barrels, and soon put that couple on Easy Street. One day the old
> man smiled and said reflectively: "But to think it was under our
> feet all the time."[1]

What would we say if one day we had an experiential realization that God has been in the depths of our being all the time? Let me tell you another story:

Once upon a time, there lived in Cracow a Jew named Eizik, son of Yekel. Devout, poor, and naive to boot, he found life more than he could handle; night and day he worried. He prayed. Day after day he begged the Lord to remember His debt-ridden and tormented servant who could go on no longer. He prayed to no avail. God seemed not to listen.

And then, one night, he had a strange dream: he saw himself swept away into a distant kingdom inside its capital, under a bridge, in the shadow of an immense palace. A voice told him: "This is Prague, this is the Vltava, and over there, the palace of the kings. Now look and look well, for under this bridge, at the spot where you are standing, there is a treasure; it is waiting for you, it is yours. Your problems are resolved."

In the morning Eizik mocked himself: dreams are very pleasant; they don't cost anything, but they don't serve any purpose either. He dismissed the entire matter from his thoughts. But that night, as soon as he closed his eyes, the same vision took hold of his mind: the capital, the palace, the bridge. And the same voice asking: "Do you want to be rich, or would you rather keep your worries?"

What nonsense, Eizik thought. Go to Prague? What an idea! He had no desire to go there. Of course, the tale does not end there. Next morning, for the third time, Eizik heard the voice: "What? You haven't left yet?"

Annoyed more than intrigued, he decided to put an end to all this, and so he started the journey. A few weeks later he arrived in Prague, famished and exhausted. He recognized the river, the bridge, the palace; it was starting all over: he was dreaming again! But no, it was not a dream. This really is strange, he thought. There was a certain spot under the bridge that looked oddly familiar. What if I tried? What do I have to lose? I should dig a hole,

take a look. But careful, not so fast. The bridge is guarded, the sol-
dier must not become suspicious. Eizik prowled the area indeci-
sively, trying to summon his courage, until he was noticed and
arrested.

The captain of the guards accused him of spying. Too fright-
ened to invent a story, he told the truth. The dreams, the worries,
the long walk begun in Cracow, the memory and the voice of that
memory. He was convinced, Eizik, that the officer would call him
a liar and order him shot. And so, he thought he was dreaming
again when the dangerous captain burst out laughing. He laughed
so hard that tears ran down his cheeks: "No, is that really why you
came from so far away? You Jews are even more stupid than I
thought! Now look at me, such as you see me here. If I were as
stupid as you, if I too listened to voices, do you know where I
would be at this very minute? In Cracow! Yes, you heard me cor-
rectly. Imagine that for weeks and weeks, there was that voice at
night telling me: 'There is a treasure waiting for you at the house
of a Cracow Jew named Eizik, son of Yekel! Yes, under the stove!'
Naturally, half the Jews there are called Eizik and the other half
Yekel! And they all have stoves! Can you see me going from house
to house tearing down all the stoves, searching for a nonexistent
treasure?"

Of course, Eizik was not punished. Of course he hurried back
home, moved the stove and, of course, he found the promised treasure. He paid his debts, married off his daughters, and as a token
of his gratitude, built a synagogue that bears his name: Eizik, son
of Yekel, a poor and pious Jew who remained pious even when he
was no longer poor.[2]

The meaning of the parable is this: The treasure, the one that
is yours, is to be found only in yourself and nowhere else. Knowledge of the absolute may be acquired only from within, never
from outside. He who thinks he must go somewhere—anywhere—
to find someone—anyone—to help him discover truth had better

stay home. Alone. That is the message of the parable. "The kingdom of God is within you" (Luke 17:21).

The experiential realization of God within, however, calls for a payment. Our Lord speaks of the kingdom of heaven, or the mystery of God revealed in himself, as "a pearl of great price." In the parable, the kingdom of heaven is like a merchant in search of pearls, who, on finding one pearl of great price, went and sold all that he had and bought it (Matt. 13:45).

In this second step the Host is presented as the pearl of great price. The guest realizes that the things he has been pursuing, such as personal ambitions, pleasure, security, power, and possessions, must be sold in order to buy that pearl. Like the rich young man to whom this scriptural passage was addressed, however, we hesitate to do that. That is why Tozan's verse for Step Two is this:

> A sleepy-eyed grandam
> Encounters herself in an old mirror.
> Clearly she sees a face
> But it doesn't resemble hers at all.
> Too bad, with a muddled head,
> She tries to recognize her reflection.

The implication of Tozan's verse is that the grandlady does see her "self" in God, but the "self" she sees is not the true "Self." And the reason she does not see the true "Self" is that her head (or her mind) is "muddled," that is to say, too preoccupied with many things.

Dr. Suzuki presents Step Two also as a straight line, but with the arrow in reverse, which means that the Host is tending to the Guest, the Host is pursuing the Guest. Again, however, we have this element of "missed connection": the Guest is too busy ("muddled") to recognize the Host's presence in her:

B ◄──────────────── A

St. Bernard would call this the step of "self-knowledge." Self-knowledge is a judgment about oneself made in faith and sincerity, because it is a question of making a judgment about oneself before God according to the truth. Self-knowledge before God makes one recognize that God is all-merciful, all-loving, and all-gracious. This knowledge is a religious awakening, an experience of God, and a consciousness of Jesus precisely as One who redeems us. Bernard writes:

> As for me, brothers, as long as I look upon myself, my eyes are filled with bitterness. But if I look up and fix my eyes on the aid of divine mercy, this happy vision of God soon tempers the bitter vision of myself. This vision of God is not a little thing. It reveals God to us as listening compassionately, as truly kind and merciful.[3]

This self-knowledge, which is nothing other than an experiential awareness of our own nothingness, also leads us to the experience of God. Bernard continues:

> If you love the Lord your God with your whole heart, whole mind, whole strength and leaping with ardent feeling beyond that love of love . . . then God indeed is experienced, although not as he truly is (a thing impossible for any creature) but rather in relation to your power to enjoy. Then you will experience your own true self as well, since you perceive that you possess nothing at all for which you love yourself, except insofar as you belong to God: you pour out upon God your whole power of loving. I repeat: you experience yourself as you are, when by the experience of love of yourself and of the feeling that you feel toward God, you discover that you are an altogether unworthy object even of your own love, except for the sake of God without whom you are nothing.[4]

This second step brings greater awareness by its dimensions of greater self-knowledge and responsibility. When we break through to awareness in the first step, it is to an inkling of an enormous safety and homecoming, like the little fish who discovers that the ocean is the very thing she is resting in. To break through on this second step brings a sense of awe and responsibility. To sense that God is in me—Host in Guest—brings with it that deep feeling, the humility that we see in the centurion who says to Jesus, "Lord, I am not worthy to receive you, but only say one word and I shall be healed" (Matt. 8:8). But at the same time, because the Host is in me, deserved or not, it increases my ardent desire to respond to this miracle—not with my usual "muddled head" but from who I really am. The urge for purity and truth grows stronger within me.

### CHAPTER 13

# Step Three:
# The Resurgence of the Host

A S THE MEDITATIVE PRACTICE around these five steps proceeds, the effect grows stronger. In this third step, the "Resurgence of the Host," the Guest, who formerly has been conscious of himself or herself as empty and poor, now begins to be aware of herself as being created in the image and likeness of God (Gen. 1:26–27) and as sharing in the divine nature (2 Pet. 1:4).

In D. T. Suzuki's diagram, the situation has now progressed to the following:

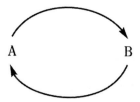

The straight lines that we found in Step One and Step Two have now become curves. This indicates that the awareness of the relationship between the Guest and the Host, between the soul and God, is no longer merely an intellectual, abstract knowledge or a cold acquaintance but rather an effective and mutual intimacy. The relationship has now become alive and blissful. The Host, or God, becomes the "ground," the "source" from which flows the

Guest's energy and life. Like the bride of the Song of Songs the soul can confidently say:

> I am my Beloved's
> and my Beloved is mine. (Song 7:11)

As this awareness grows in our soul, we begin to feel that God is truly living in us and we are truly living in God. That is why this step is called "The Resurgence of the Host in the Guest," or "The Coming of God into the Soul." Here we begin to realize the word of Our Lord:

> If you love me
> you will keep my word,
> and my Father will love you,
> and we will come to you
> and make our home with you. (John 14:23)

The person at this step starts to feel at home with God, to feel God's intimacy as a mutual responsivity. The attraction of their mutual love is experienced with equal force and a kind of continuous circulation, as expressed in the following phrase:

> Going-to within the Coming-from
> Coming-from within the Going-to.

In practice the meditator at this stage is advised to "feel" within oneself the interplay of this expression: "Going-to within the Coming-from, and Coming-from within the Going-to." There is a livingness hidden in this expression. A meditative awareness of it will make this livingness felt. The relationship between God and the soul at this stage is very alive.

Tozan describes Step Three in the following verse:

> Within nothingness there is a path
> Leading away from the dust of the world.
> Even if you observe the taboo

> On the present emperor's name
> You will surpass that eloquent one of yore
> Who silenced every tongue.

Why, "within nothingness," is "a path leading away from the dust of the world?" It is because in this step the self is more aware of being empty, being nothing in the sight of God, and so is more responsive to the spirit, more open to God. An example of this situation is the Blessed Virgin. She can "magnify the Lord" (in the words of her beautiful Hymn of Praise in Luke 1:4), because the Lord has "looked upon her in her lowliness." The virgin birth is possible because Mary is found to be totally open to God in love.

Speaking of the birth of God in the soul, the medieval mystic John Tauler writes:

> The soul must go out. She must travel away from herself, above herself. This is to say we must deny ourselves, our own will and all desire and activity of our own. There must be nothing left in us but a pure intention toward God; no will to be or become or obtain anything for ourselves. We must exist only to make a place for him, the highest innermost place, where he may do his work; there, when we are no longer putting ourselves in his way, he can be born in us. For if two people are to become one, one of them must be passive while the other acts. Nothing can be receptive until it is empty and passive and free.[1]

Now the call to the "wedding banquet" becomes more urgent:

> Behold the bridegroom comes,
> go out to meet him! (Matt. 25:6)

Jesus likens the kingdom of God to a leaven that a woman hid in three measures of flour until the whole mass was raised (Luke 13:21). The implication is that the contemplative experience can only happen "inside," within the depths of our being. As long as the leaven is on the outside, the dough is powerless to rise; the leaven has to get inside. The Host must act from within the Guest. It is not only the Guest who longs for union with the Host; the Host himself seeks this union with a sense of urgency:

> Look, I am standing at the door, knocking.
> If anyone hears me and opens the door,
> I will enter and sup with that one. (Rev. 3:20)

Mary Magdalene's encounter with the risen Christ is symbolic of what happens in Step Three. Mary, a woman, was the first person who witnessed and experienced the resurrection of Christ. The essence of "resurrection" and the mutual experience of the event corresponds to the state described in "The Resurgence of the Host." When Jesus appeared to Mary Magdalene in the garden on the first day of the week (John 20:11–18), he called out to her: "Mary!" In calling her by name, Christ woke in her the feelings and the emotions of her own inner power, both psychic and spiritual. In other words, he raised Mary to a new awareness of herself. Her whole being became alive to the power of Christ's risen body, which now becomes the life-giving spirit (1 Cor. 15:44). Before Our Lord called Mary by her first name, she was at a complete loss; in the midst of her tears and despair she thought that the man standing before her was a gardener. But as soon as he spoke her name, she recognized him and embraced him in an ecstasy of reunion.

Let us move on to St. Bernard. Bernard uses the symbol of the bridegroom for the Host and the bride for the Guest. He describes the situation in Step Three as the "loving descent" of the bridegroom to the bride, and the "ecstatic ascent" of the bride to the bridegroom. The soul desires an exclusive encounter with God in her inmost being, and God penetrates the soul swiftly as the word penetrates the ears without sound. Bernard writes:

> I will try to express, using the most suitable words that I can
> muster, this ecstatic ascent of the purified mind to God, and the

loving descent of God into the soul, submitting "spiritual truth to spiritual people" (1 Cor. 2:13). . . .

One who is so disposed and so beloved will by no means be content with either that manifestation of the Bridegroom given to the many in the world of creatures or to few in visions and dreams. By special privilege the soul wishes to welcome God down from heaven into her inmost heart, into her deepest love. She wishes to have the One she desires present to her, not in bodily form, but by an inward fusion, not by appearing externally but by laying hold of her within. It is beyond question that the vision is all the more delightful, the more inward it is, rather than external. This is the Word who penetrates without sound, who is effective though not pronounced, who wins the affections without sounding in the ears. God's face, though itself without form, is the source of all forms. It does not dazzle the eyes of the body but gladdens the watchful heart. Its pleasure is in the gift of love, not in the handsome appearance of the lover.[2]

The journey of the soul to God and the coming of God into the soul are beautifully articulated. The directness of the experience renders it inexpressible in words, so Bernard gives the words a meaning that is derived from the experience, rather than expecting the words to convey a meaning that their limited definitions cannot bear of themselves. Bernard appeals to "spiritual people" to abandon all external and familiar forms and to yield to the advance of the Bridegroom within the soul through the directness of love—no thoughts, no sounds, no external forms, and no duration or time. Love is the direct encounter of the soul with the Bridegroom. The self is left behind in the ecstasy of love. This is too much for the external senses to endure or prolong. The experience, in fact, seems to be very brief, very rare, and very private, but all else pales before it. Bernard writes:

It is good to save many souls, but there is far more pleasure in going aside to be with the Word. But when does this happen, and for how long? It is sweet intercourse, but lasts a short time and is experienced rarely![3]

Bernard's sudden disappointment is the result of the intensity of the joy. The world of the senses and the emotions cannot endure for long the overflow of contemplative joy that the experience gives. There is a sort of overcharge on the lower faculties when they become aware of the direct experience of "The Resurgence of the Host," or the visit of the Bridegroom:

> But when does this happen?
> And how long does it last?
> It is sweet intercourse,
> But it lasts only a short time,
> And is experienced but rarely.[4]

### CHAPTER 14

# Step Four:
# Mutual Interpenetration
# of Guest and Host

A S WE MAKE PROGRESS in our meditative practice, the effect grows stronger and stronger. This involves an increased responsiveness to the Holy Spirit. Now the Guest is in all respects one with the Host, so that there is no other desire. This would show itself in ordinary life when the Guest has no longer any planning for his or her own separate self, but only proceeds with thinking or acting when there is a call. In D. T. Suzuki's diagram, the situation is now as follows:

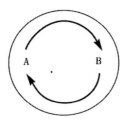

The Host and the Guest no longer move around one another but progress toward a mutual interpenetration. The two arrows are now *within* the circle, indicating that the interaction—or the movement of the Host and the Guest—is no longer vague and impersonal but creative and inexhaustible. In the awareness of the individual soul—the Guest—the limits of the "self" have been left behind and no longer seem to circumscribe life. A new kind of "self" surrounds the movement, which belongs as much to the Host as to the Guest. Tozan's verse on this step is:

> The arrival at Mutual Interpenetration:
> When two blades cross points,
> There is no need to withdraw.
> The master swordsman
> Is like the lotus blooming in the fire.
> Such a one has in and of oneself
> A heaven-soaring spirit.

"When two blades cross points" means that in this step one perceives the mutuality and reciprocity of love between God and the soul. This sense of "oneness" is characteristic of love. The soul "knows God as she is known by God."

To the soul thus brought into such intimacy of love, God is no longer an impersonal God but rather extremely personal—even transpersonal. The Infinite Being, in a love without any limits whatsoever, is now experienced as sharing this love with the soul. The supreme, desirable God is now experienced as the "desiring God," who is giving himself to the soul.

In the language of Tozan, the soul is "like the lotus blooming in the fire." This means that the soul, on encountering the fire of God's love, becomes brighter in color and purer in fragrance. Such a soul "has in and of herself a heaven-soaring spirit."

As a symbol of this level of intimacy with God, we could turn to the event when the angel Gabriel came to Mary to announce the mystery of the incarnation (Luke 1:26). Reflecting on this "angelic salutation," Bernard writes:

> Mary was so full of the Divinity dwelling within her corporeally, so full of the Holy Spirit, as to conceive by him. God went forth from the heavenly tent and rejoiced as a giant to run the divine course, with ardent affection, in search of the Virgin whom God loved.[1]

In his comments on the most famous verse in the Song of Songs–"I am my Beloved's and my Beloved is mine"–Bernard writes:

> There can be no doubt that the mutual love of the Bridegroom and Bride burns as a fire in the furnace. And in that reciprocity of affection we behold the supreme happiness of the one and the amazing kindness of the other. This is a secret which no one can pretend to understand fully, except those who by the perfect purity of their souls and bodies have deserved to experience something similar in themselves. For it is a mystery of love. Hence it is not by discourse or reason that we are to attain to it but by the conformity of will.[2]

This "conformity of will" is Bernard's expression for the direct experience of a mutual embrace. Unlike the agreement of the mind that is mediated through language, the embrace of love is direct and perfectly intimate. In Sermon 83 on the Song of Songs Bernard writes:

> It is by conformity of love that the soul is wedded to the Word, when, namely, loving even as she is loved, she exhibits herself in her will to be conformed to him to whom she is already conformed in her nature. There, if she loves him perfectly, she becomes his Bride. . . . This is in truth the alliance of spiritual marriage. But it is too little to call it an alliance; it is rather an embrace. Surely we have here a spiritual embrace when the same likes and dislikes make one spirit out of two. Nor is there any occasion to fear the inequality of the two persons lest this cause some defect in the harmony of wills since love knows nothing of reverence. Love means an exercise of affection, not an exhibition of honor. . . . Love is all-sufficient for itself. Wherever love comes, it subjugates and renders captive to itself all the other affections. Consequently the soul that loves, simply loves and knows nothing else except love. The Word is indeed One who deserves to be honored, admired and wondered at, yet he is better pleased to be loved.[3]

Thus, Bernard describes love not as an option in pursuing the contemplative experience but as the essence of the experience; this level of love is not subject to the limitations of discursive thought, but is direct and all-absorbing. It subjects to itself all other faculties, including the very awareness of self. In this sense it is that "one thing necessary" spoken about by Our Lord in St. Luke's Gospel:

> In the course of their journey, Jesus came to a village, and a woman named Martha welcomed him into her house. She had a sister called Mary, who sat at the Lord's feet and listened to him speaking. Now Martha, who was distracted with all the serving, said: "Lord, do you not care that my sister is leaving me to do the serving all by myself? Please tell her to help me!" But the Lord answered: "Martha, Martha, you worry and fret about so many things, yet few are needed; indeed, only one. It is Mary who has chosen the better part. It is not to be taken from her." (Luke 10:38–42)

Mary seemed to grasp the key to the contemplative experience for the Lord affirmed that she had chosen the better part and that no one should take it away from her. Notice how Christ referred to this as "the one thing necessary."

An old Chinese legend points to this same "one thing necessary" and helps us to understand Our Lord's reference. The legend goes as follows:

> In ninth century China there was a hermit named Gutei. Before Gutei had any contemplative experience he lived alone at the foot of a mountain. It was a quiet place, good for meditation, and Gutei spent a lot of time sitting in his hut. Outside, the autumn leaves were stirred by the wind and fell to the ground. The first-quarter moon shed her dim light. A figure showed itself from the dark and entered the hut. This was the nun Jissai, dressed in priestly clothes, with a broad hat and pilgrim's staff.

According to the custom in China, when two people meet, they take off their hats and greet each other. Jissai, however, did not follow the proper decorum. She was discourteous enough to walk around Gutei three times without removing her hat; then, standing straight in front of Gutei, she said, "If you show me the key to the contemplative experience I will remove my hat."

Gutei was, however, at a complete loss for words, since his spiritual eyes had not been opened. Jissai once more walked around Gutei and again asked her question. Finding that Gutei still could not return an answer, she began to leave. Gutei said, "It is already dark, why don't you stay here for the night?" Jissai replied, "Show me the key to contemplative experience and I will stay." Gutei said nothing, and Jissai walked out into the night.[4]

Suppose the nun Jissai asked you the same question. Could you give her the answer? Unless you had already passed through Step Four, you would not be able to satisfy Jissai.

According to the myth, that night Gutei tossed and turned in his couch, saying to himself,

"What a useless fellow I am! This will never do. Tomorrow I will leave this mountain and set out in search of a teacher who can give me instruction." However, as Gutei dozed, his guardian angel appeared in a dream and said to him, "Do not leave this mountain. A living master is coming to visit you. He will give you instruction." After this dream, Gutei decided to remain in his hermitage and wait for this master to come.

Sure enough, within a few days Tenryu Osho came to visit his hut. Gutei told him the whole story and asked him, "What is the key to the contemplative experience?" No sooner had Gutei said this than Tenryu raised one finger. Gutei suddenly gained the insight; he discovered the key to the contemplative experience.[5]

Master Tenryu's gesture of raising one finger as an answer to Gutei's question is significant. It is the same as Jesus' saying to Martha that "one thing is necessary" and that Mary had chosen the better part. Even in the Gospel, the symbol of the "finger of God" is used to describe the action of the Holy Spirit. St. Luke tells us how Jesus uses the "finger of God" to cast out demons (Luke 11:20). The monastic hymn for the First Vespers of the Feast of Pentecost uses the same image of the "finger of God" to apply to the Holy Spirit:

> Thou who are the Paraclete,
> Thou best gift of God above;
> The living Spring, the living Love.
> Thou who are Sevenfold in the Grace,
> Finger of God's right hand;
> His promise, teaching little ones
> to speak and understand.

In his comments on the legend of Gutei, Zen master Mumon Ekai (1183–1260) observes:

> The enlightenment of Gutei is not in the finger. If you see through this, then master Tenryu, Gutei, and you, and indeed the whole universe are all run through with one skewer.[6]

The unity that pervades the whole universe is expressed in the lifting up of one finger. The finger is not the unity, but the Unity is in the finger. If the key to the contemplative experience is not in the finger, then where is it? We are told not to be misled by the word "finger." What is it that is in front of you? What is it that stands behind you? At the level of the senses, the finger is seen in front of you. The self tries to grasp the concreteness of this thing and identifies with what the mind or senses reveal about it.

But this is not the "one thing necessary." This effort of the "self" to grasp and hold on to this concrete world must be let go, or the vision of the "many" will obscure the inner eye that allows one to see the "one thing necessary." "Martha, Martha, you are concerned about 'many' things, but one thing is necessary." The self identifies with the "many," which must be cast away and left behind. This self must die. Then our inner eye will be opened and we will be able to see the "finger of God" in everything. Our contemplative experience is with the One. Whether we are standing or sitting, coming or going, it is all nothing but the "finger of God" come upon us. This is our key and it will not be taken from us. All else will pass away, but this will not pass away. Here is another poem from an Eastern master that illustrates the significance of the "one finger":

> Korei raised his finger with no effort.
> And lo! The great ridge of Mount A was split in two!
> And let the great river run through
> The range of the mountain.[7]

How dynamically and amazingly the "one finger" works! It is the power of the Holy Spirit. The work of the Spirit is creative and mysterious. As Korei's finger breaks a mountain in two and allows a river to flow through the rift, so the Holy Spirit opens the thick blindness that stands in front of our inner eyes and allows the river of the One to flow through the "many." The Holy Spirit is the one who shows us the key to the contemplative experience. The Holy Spirit, in fact, *is* that key. It is the Spirit who brings us to Christ and reveals Christ to us. Our Lord assures us, "The Spirit will make known to you all that I have told you" (John 14:26). The Holy Spirit is the unity, the mutual embrace between the Host and the Guest, between God and the soul.

There is yet another puzzling anecdote that points toward this Step Four:

> A traveling monk once asked an old woman which way he should take to go to the Mountain of Wisdom. The old woman answered: "Go straight ahead!" But when the monk had taken a few steps, she remarked: "He may look like a fine monk, but he goes off like that!"

Now the Mountain of Wisdom was the holy mountain. From ancient times many wise contemplative monks had lived on this mountain. Monks in training would make their pilgrimage to it. The old woman lived at the foot of the Mountain of Wisdom, where she probably ran a tea house by the side of the road that led to the mountain. Whenever a traveling monk would ask her: "Which way should I go to get to the Mountain of Wisdom?" she would never say to the monk, "Turn to the East," or "Turn to the West." She would always say, "Go straight ahead!" But then, when the monk would actually turn and begin to take steps toward the Mountain, she would look at him with scorn and repeat: "This monk again! He may look like a fine monk, but he is an awkward monk!"

Now the way to the Mountain of Wisdom is the way to Truth. Wisdom is within oneself. As Jesus said: "The kingdom of God is within you." If you are really seeking the kingdom of God, the one thing necessary, you will not waste your steps walking this way or that way. If you do, the woman will tell you, "You look like a fine monk, but really you are an awkward monk!" You will never get to the Mountain of Wisdom until you are enlightened from within. What is the use of looking for it outside of oneself? As Jesus said to the Samaritan woman:

> The water that I shall give
> Will turn into a spring of water inside you
> Welling up into eternal life. (John 4:14)

The road to wisdom is the interior journey. The external road to the Holy Mountain is only a symbol. But once our "self" can be freed from attachment to the external road and actually begin the interior journey, the steps become more direct and lead us to the Host, who receives us and who, amazingly, comes to meet us. We no longer need to go to the mountain. The mountain has come to us. The mountain "splits in two," and rivers of living water flow in between. Distance is no more, and events do not succeed one another.

Our Lord, too, spoke of Wisdom in terms of the mountain. He told the Samaritan woman:

> Believe me, woman, the hour is coming when neither on this mountain nor in Jerusalem will you worship the Father. You worship what you do not know; we worship what we know, for salvation is from the Jews. But the hour is coming, and now is, when the true worshipers will worship the Father in spirit and in truth, for such the Father seeks to worship him. God is spirit, and those who worship him must worship in spirit and in truth. (John 4:21-24)

So it was with our monk looking for the Mountain of Wisdom. Not realizing his inner self, the monk followed the words of the woman literally and headed off toward the mountain that was "straight ahead" but outside of himself. The woman could not help but laugh at him saying: "He may look like a fine monk but he goes off like that!"

So also with Jesus, saying to the Samaritan woman: "You worship what you do not know." Is Jesus also saying to us: "You worship what you do not know"?

Who is the old woman? What does she mean when she tells the traveling monks to "go straight ahead"? Why does she laugh when they follow her directions exteriorly and walk off like that? These are profound questions and require that our inner eyes be opened before we are able to grasp the meaning. But when we do, we have also grasped the key to contemplative experience.

In a letter to Pope Eugene III, St. Bernard wrote:

> We should not be content to meditate on God in creation only. We must enter our own inward depth. By special privilege the soul wants to welcome him down from heaven into her inmost heart, into her deepest love. She wants to have the One she desires pres-

ent to her not in bodily form but by inward infusion, not by appearing externally but by laying hold of her within.[8]

And in an Advent sermon Bernard is very clear:

This "going inward" is nothing distant, nothing esoteric, nothing complicated. It is the depth and lucidity of the Gospel, because "The kingdom of God is within you." It does not behoove you, O creature like God, to cross the seas, to penetrate the clouds or to climb the Alps in search of God. No great journey is necessary for you. Seek no further than your own soul, there will you find your God.[9]

### CHAPTER 15

# Step Five:
# Unity Attained

A T STEP FOUR THE GUEST REALIZED oneness with the Host. This oneness with the Host involves oneness with all, so that the realization includes everything and everyone. Tozan's expression for Step Four is "the dewdrop slips into the shining sea," but in Step Five, "The universe grows I."[1]

Here is the true destination of the contemplative journey. Attaining this unity with Christ, the person embraces everyone, both friends and foes; he or she realizes the truth of the Chinese proverb that says: "People of the four oceans are brothers." Thus Master Tozan's verse:

> Unity attained:
> Who dares to equal one
> Who falls into neither being nor non-being?
> All people want to leave
> The current of ordinary life,
> But he, after all, comes back
> To sit among coals and ashes.

This is the state of perfect unity wherein the Host and the Guest have no more individual traces and are but one undivided whole. This state is without comparison, and so Tozan is correct when he says that "such a one has no equal." While most people want to leave the sea of suffering of ordinary life, the person who has reached this state of "Unity Attained" comes back to the marketplace to bestow benefit on everybody. D. T. Suzuki expresses "Unity Attained" by the famous T'ai-chi-T'u, or the Yin-Yang symbol, the diagram of the Supreme Ultimate.

The created universe carries Yin at its back
And the Yang in the front.
Through the union of the pervading Principles
It reaches Harmony.[2]

Thus, with the attainment of Step Five, union of the Guest and the Host has been attained as a state of rest, which is really a dynamic equilibrium. In Step Four, union is desired and sought after with the great longing of love because it has begun to happen. Now the goal has been reached and there is satiation, enjoyment with rest and security. The spiritual marriage is now consummated and enjoyed.

It might be good at this point to remind ourselves that we are only speaking analogously when we use this type of language. The limits and the complexities that human language imposes are more of a barrier to realizing the contemplative experience than they are a means of discovering it. When we have discovered our direct contemplative experience, these poor words can serve as a reminder because of the presence of the "One" that is always present in the concreteness of the "many."

Before we are introduced experientially to this union of the Guest and the Host, the words that describe the experience will only serve to confound our understanding. But be of good cheer! Do not be discouraged by this aspect of the truth, because it is only the way to growth. The fetus in the womb would never choose to experience the trauma of birth and the necessity of breathing on its own because it has no inkling of what it is destined for. But once it comes to experience living and breathing on its own, the fetus would no longer choose to return to the comfort (and ignorance) of the womb. So also with our birth into the spiritual life. We have no way of reducing the spiritual to the level of the sensible, which would enable our sensible nature to form a desire for it. Nor can we reduce the spiritual to reason or to concepts, for these are also a limited form of reality.

If the Guest, in all the restrictions of its limited forms of existence, is to enter into union with the Host who is unlimited, this must come about by the act of love which the Host shows to the Guest. Though the Host may manifest his love by signs/sacraments, by words/language, by deeds/miracles, still it is through the spiritual faculty of faith that we must respond. And as all spiritual masters know, faith goes the "way of darkness." It chooses that which the senses cannot touch, the emotions cannot feel, the imagination cannot conceive, and the reasoning mind itself cannot will. The spiritual faculty of faith alone is capable of engaging the unlimited truth directly. This is the urgency of the cry of Jesus: "When the Son of Man comes, do you think he will find faith?" Faith is the key to our contemplative experience, and love is the experience.

In Step Five, the Guest completes the journey; the seeker attains his or her object and becomes one with it. There is no more distinction here between object and subject, between the knowing subject and the known object.

In our normal way of thinking and perceiving, the presence of a proper object to our faculties is that which makes us realize our self as subject. For instance, a piece of fruit on the table before me is not a sensible object to me until I gaze upon it with my eyes and realize that I am seeing a piece of fruit. Once that is done, I know myself as someone who has seen a piece of fruit. I still do not know myself as one who knows the smell, touch, and taste of this piece of fruit until I have actually brought the fruit into contact with each of these senses. Then I know myself as the one who has touched, smelled, and tasted the piece of fruit. This is simple to see, but it is the fact that the *object* is that which makes me a subject that is the point we are noticing. I know myself by the act of coming in contact with the appropriate object of my sense faculties. So also with my emotions, my imagination, and my intellect. Initial contact with their proper objects will show myself as subject. It is not the other way around. I do not first know myself as subject and then go looking for objects. This will also be true with my contemplative experience. I will not have contemplative experience until I have had direct contact with its proper object. I can no more cause contemplative experience with my intellect or my mind or with the language and concepts that my mind has fashioned than I can do calculus with my taste buds. Oranges taste sweet to my mouth, but mental calculations don't even register there.

Ideas and concepts are wonderful to the mind, but the unlimited love of God doesn't register except in the higher faculty of faith. We must not be dismayed by this, but embrace it as part of the journey by which we go to God, step by step.

When the limits of the Guest begin to fall away in the embrace with the Host, then the awareness of the self as a subject begins to change. In fact, the change is so radical and complete that the self as subject seems to undergo death. There is something in our awareness that foretells the necessity of this death of self, and this pre-awareness stirs up a huge unnamed fear. In this sense, it is true that, "the fear of the Lord is the first stage of wisdom" (Prov. 1:7). The awareness of ourselves as the subject that has been in contact with all the objects of our lifelong experience begins to fade and die out. All the objects are still there, but we as subjects are no longer defined by them. They are no longer our limit. Instead of "someone" who is looking at "something," we seem to be moving into a state of "pure awareness" where there is no contact between the Guest and the Host. There is no contact because there is no separation. The union is direct. It is not mediated through language or feelings or sensations. It just is. We are now only aware that we are; we are no longer aware that we have.

In his description of the state of "Unity Attained," Bernard combines Step Four and Step Five into what he calls "the fourth degree of love." In this single step, the soul finds herself completely lost in the Word. Here is the unity of love. Here is the *consummatum est* (John 19:30). There is nothing more in the journey for the soul to expect or find wanting:

> In this contemplation the soul is sometimes rapt in ecstasy and withdrawn from the bodily senses, and so completely absorbed in admiration of the Word that she loses consciousness of herself. This happens when, under the attraction of the Word's ineffable sweetness, she steals away, as it were, from herself, or rather is ravished and slips away from herself to enjoy the Word.[3]

As would be expected, we find Bernard describing this stage in terms of love between the Word and the soul. This love culminates in an intimate and rapturous union. When Bernard comes to describe the delight of that union, he uses the image of a silent song whose melody is heard only between the lovers:

> Only the touch of the Spirit [cf. 1 John 2:27] can inspire a song like this, and only personal experience can unfold its meaning. Let those who are versed in the mystery revel in it. Let all others burn with desire not so much to know as to attain to this experience.

For it is thrilling on the lips but in the inward heart it is a pulsing of delight, a harmony not of voices but of wills. It is a melody not heard on the streets; these notes do not sound where crowds assemble. Only the singer hears it and the one to whom he sings— the lover and the beloved. For it is a nuptial song telling of chaste souls in loving embrace, of their wills in sweet concord, of the mutual exchange of the heart's affections.[4]

In his famous treatise *On Loving God* (*De Diligendo Deo*), Bernard waxes eloquent about the soul who has reached this state of the journey:

Happy the soul who has attained to this fourth degree of love. She no longer loves even herself except for God. . . . When this sort of affection is felt, inebriated with divine love, the mind may forget itself and become in its own eyes a broken dish, hastening towards God and clinging to him, becoming one with him in spirit, saying: "My flesh and heart may fail, but God is the strength of my heart and my portion forever."[5]

Bernard goes on to describe how the "self" suffers a form of dying and the bride finds herself lost in the Bridegroom. This is her true contemplative experience. She knows herself to be one with the God who has loved her:

I would say that one is blessed and holy to whom it has been given to experience something like this, so rare in life, even if it be but once and for the space of a moment. To lose yourself as if you no longer existed, to cease completely to be aware of yourself, to reduce yourself to nothing, is not a human sentiment but a divine experience.[6]

The Eastern masters have described Step Five in various ways, but again the image of birth and death often comes up. One master has said that Unity Attained is like "coming to life again after you have lost your hold and fallen over the edge of a precipice to your death." For another, "The moment of Unity Attained is the moment when you die the Great Death." Still another has said: "It is the state in which the 'Great Life' clearly manifests itself."

In this stage Bernard perceives the contemplative experience as "ecstasy" and associates the images of repose, sleep, and even death with this ecstasy. This special sleep that the bride experiences in the suspension of her sensory awareness is a death that at the same time is full of a new and wondrous life:

> Consider therefore that the bride has retired to this solitude. Therefore, overcome by the loveliness of the place, she sleeps sweetly within the arms of her Bridegroom in the ecstasy of Spirit.[7] It is a slumber which is vital and watchful, which enlightens the heart, drives away death, and communicates eternal life. For it is a genuine sleep that does not stupefy the mind but transports it. And—I say it without hesitation—it is a death. For the Apostle Paul, in praising those still living in the flesh, spoke thus: "For you have died, and your life is hidden with Christ in God."[8]

In another place Bernard writes:

> I can be guilty of no absurdity when I describe the ecstasy of the Spouse as a kind of death, not the death which terminates life but that which gives us freedom. . . . For as often as the spouse is transported out of herself by some holy and irresistible attraction, just so the mental exultation and ravishment seem to be so great as to lift her above the common and usual mode of thinking and feeling. . . . Would to God that I could often endure a death of this kind.[9]

But, as it has been said, this death of the soul in ecstatic union with her Bridegroom is also a form of birth and of coming to life:

> In this kind of birth the soul leaves even her bodily senses and is separated from them, so that, in her awareness of the Word, she is not aware of herself. This happens when the mind is enraptured by the unutterable sweetness of the Word, so that she withdraws or rather is transported and escapes from herself to enjoy the Word.[10]

Etienne Gilson made note of the fact that Bernard had a great love for the Passion of Christ. He remarked, however, that this love for the Passion was only a vehicle leading toward a higher love!

> The sensible affection for Christ was always presented by Bernard as love of a relatively inferior order. This is so precisely because of its sensible character, for love is of a purely spiritual order. By right, the soul should be able to enter directly into union in virtue of its spiritual powers with God who is purely spirit. We have it from Bernard that he was much given to the practice of this sensible love at the outset of his conversion; later on he was to consider it an advance to have passed beyond it; not, that is to say, to have forgotten it, but to have added another dimension which outweighed it, as the rational and spiritual outweighs the carnal. Nevertheless, this beginning is always a summit.[11]

Gilson's observation is certainly in line with Bernard's view. For Bernard, meditation on the Passion and the Resurrection always prepares the soul for the visit of the Word or for the contemplative experience. Bernard wrote:

> If we wish to have Christ as a frequent Guest, we must ever have our hearts fortified with unfailing testimonials both of his mercy in dying and of his power in rising from death.[12] Where Christ perceives that the grace of his Passion or the glory of his Resurrection is the subject of diligent meditation, there straightaway he is present with eagerness and joy.[13] . . . The soul longs to add to the fruits of the Passion which she has plucked from the tree of the Cross the flowers of the Resurrection whose fragrance especially allures the Beloved to visit her again.[14]

Bernard burst into joy when he realized this step of Unity Attained. "Blessed is One!" is the exclamation of joy he uttered after emerging from his deep contemplative ecstasy, having been momentarily lost in the divine immensity. It is the ultimate word, the summing up of all he could say about the ineffable blessedness which the soul enjoys through being unified with God in a most intimate friendship. In his eighty-third sermon on the Song of Songs he writes:

> This is truly a blessed state when the soul is united with God the Word in a nuptial union. This is nothing but the final crown of all our love for God in this life. Happy the soul to whom it has been given to experience and embrace such surpassing delight! This spiritual embrace is nothing else than a chaste and holy love, a love sweet and pleasant, a love perfectly serene and perfectly pure, a love that is mutual, intimate and strong, a love that joins two, not in one flesh but in one spirit.[15] . . . Perhaps there are some of you who would now like an explanation of what it is like to enjoy the Word in this way. Had I been privileged sometimes to experience that favor, do you suppose it would be possible for me to describe the ineffable?[16]

The sense of well-being and happiness brought about by this state of contemplative experience is not a mere consciousness of something; it is a fusion in the innermost depths of the soul, from which an awareness of some ineffable good and an experience of deep joy overflow. As D. T. Suzuki observes:

> The feeling of exultation which inevitably accompanies enlightenment is due to the fact that it is the breaking-up of the restriction imposed upon one as an individual being. This breaking up is not a mere negative incident but a quite positive experience— fraught with significance because it means an infinite expansion of the individual. The general feeling, though we are not always conscious of it, which characterizes the routine functions of consciousness, is that of restriction and dependence, because consciousness itself is the outcome of two forces conditioning or restricting one another. Enlightenment, on the contrary, consists essentially in doing away with the opposition found between any two terms. Enlightenment is to realize the Unconscious or the

Transcendental which goes beyond opposition. To be released from this tension, therefore, causes one to feel raised above conflicting forces and intensely exalted. Thus the individual person, who is a wandering outcast, maltreated everywhere, not only by others but by himself, inexplicably finds that one is the possessor of all wealth and power that is ever attainable in this world by a mortal being; if this experience does not give one a high feeling of self-glorification, what could?[17]

## PART FOUR

# Contemplative Experience
# and Beyond

### CHAPTER 16

# Contemplative Experience and the Active Life

THE QUESTION ARISES: What does a person do once he or she has arrived at the stage of Unity Attained? Is the person who is resting in the mutual exchange of love with God no longer interested in the everyday pursuits of our limited world? This does not seem to be the case. In this final stage of the contemplative journey, the person can rest in God and still be engaged in the activities and works of charity or the service to his or her neighbor. It is important to know that the stage of Unity Attained does not invalidate all our other commitments and, even more wonderfully, that we can keep them in a new way, with our heart and mind still completely centered in God.

This is the state in which St. Bernard frequently was found as his contemplative experience deepened. William of St. Thierry, an intimate friend and biographer of St. Bernard, noted that:

> Bernard's soul was flooded with such peaceful grace that, while he gave himself completely to the work at hand, his mind was completely taken up with God.[1]

Since Bernard was a mystic, we tend to think that his only concern must have been prayer and contemplation. This is far from the truth. In Sermon 57 on the Song of Songs Bernard wrote:

> It is characteristic of true and pure contemplation that when the mind is ardently aglow with God's love, it is sometimes so filled

with the zeal and the desire to gather for God those who will love him with equal abandon, that it gladly forgoes contemplative leisure for the endeavor of preaching. And then with its desire at least partially satisfied it returns to its leisure with an eagerness proportionate to its successful interruption, after which, it hastens to add to its conquests with renewed strength and experienced zeal.[2]

Bernard advised his monks to pray and appeal to God that God might show them a right balance between service, prayer, and contemplation. It must be admitted that confusion can result from playing contemplation and action off against each other and favoring the "duty" of service over the "attraction" of contemplation. Activities of service can actually be a *hindrance* in the journey toward God, and it requires discernment to know when they are part of the journey and when they have become obstacles on the journey. The one who marches off in search of the Mountain of Wisdom may look like a fine monk, as the woman at the foot of the mountain remarks, but he is only running away from the interior life and not "going straight ahead"; in such a case the best advice would be to stop running and submit more deeply to the interior union.

But once the goal of the journey is attained, and the union with the Host is direct and without the limits of duration, location, emotions, or concepts, then the blessing of that divine union overflows and penetrates all the other levels of our being and action. In either case, the activities seem to be the same, but the "subject" from whom they originate is infinitely different. Though the activities are the actions of the Guest, the source of the action is the resurgence of the Host within the Guest. So Bernard advises his monks to pray for a right balance:

It is fitting to the soul as "friend of the Bridegroom" to work for the advantage of her Bridegroom; as a "Dove" to pray with sighs and supplications; as his "Beautiful One" to clothe herself with the beauty of divine contemplation.[3]

Bernard maintains that any one of us who keeps a similar balance will, in like manner, be greeted as a "Friend," consoled as a "Dove," and embraced as a "Beauty."[4]

Any activity can deepen our contemplative experience as long as it is done with a contemplative attitude. Some years ago I had the joy of welcoming Mother Teresa of Calcutta into our monastery at Spencer. During my lovely exchange with Mother, I asked her a naive question: "Mother, being so busy working all day and traveling all over the world non-stop, where in the world do you find time to pray and to contemplate?"

With her loving eyes, she looked at me and said, "Father, my contemplation is when I touch the sick, when I embrace the dying child, when I wash the wounds of a leper. Jesus told us that whenever you do these things to the least of my brothers and sisters, you do it to me; and I know Jesus always tells the truth. To me the dying child or the lepers are only Jesus in disguise."

Let us seek, by prayer and ardent desire, for a charity that will bring us to that spiritual maturity in Christ which will unite both action and contemplation in our own souls.

### CHAPTER 17

# Mary, the Model of Contemplative Experience

I HAVE DISCUSSED THUS FAR THE TOUCHSTONES of my own contemplative experience, namely, the meditative reading of Sacred Scripture, the study of St. Bernard's mystical writings, an immersion in the wisdom of the Eastern masters, and above all the immersion in the mystery of Christ in the Eucharist. In this chapter I would like to present the last, but by no means the least, of my touchstones for contemplative experience: the Blessed Virgin Mary, model of contemplative union with God.

If we can say that contemplative experience is an "experiential realization of intimate union with God," we can say, then, that Mary's entire life was a constant contemplative experience and continues to be! Because she incessantly lives her daily, ordinary life in intimate union with God, Mary holds a special place of honor in Cistercian communities. She is our patron. All our monasteries are dedicated to her and bear her image in a stained glass window or statue. The final act of each monastic day is to gather before her image and sing the "Salve Regina"–"Hail, Holy Queen." This devotion to Mary is not old-fashioned or sentimental. Monks have long realized that Mary bears within her the fullness of the contemplative experience, and she is our model and guide for contemplative life. She also bears within her the fullness of the *human* experience. As a symbol of the eternal feminine, she holds the key to our own inner integration and to the mystery that must be accomplished in each one of us: to be born again, "not of blood nor of the will of the flesh nor of the will of man, but of God" (John 1:13).

### *Mary, the Symbol of the Feminine in a Human Being*

Mary is a model of the soul in the attitude of contemplation and loving surrender to God. When the angel Gabriel announced to Mary that she would conceive and bear a son by the Holy Spirit, she opened her total being to God, saying, "Behold the handmaid of the Lord! Be it done to me according to your word" (Luke 1:38). In complete openness to God's will, she surrendered herself to God as a *woman,* allowing God's seed to fall into her womb. In *Mary: The Womb of God,* George Maloney wrote:

> Mary the contemplative is the archetypal symbol of the feminine in every human being. We come alive as Christians, the Church becomes the dynamic, living Body of Christ, when we yield to the feminine in us. The womb of Mary powerfully describes to us at the deepest reaches of our unconscious that primeval hunger that God has implanted within all of us to circumvent, surround, enfold the wild, unpossessible, transcendent God.[1]

Eastern psychology holds that the blending of the two principles, the Yang (or masculine) and the Yin (or feminine), makes the integrated human person. In a modern rephrasing of this ancient wisdom, our relationship with God is also seen as a blending of these two principles. L. Beirnaert in *Mystique et Conscience* insisted: "It is the psyche, the anima, the soul that makes contact with God . . . and that is in a feminine relationship with God."[2]

In the same vein, Matthew Kelty makes this startling statement in *Flute Solo:*

No man is only man. The human race is not just man. How can we relate to God without reference to woman? And how can we come to know the whole Christ if we have no woman through whom to do so? And to assume that we can relate to the Church, our Mother, Christ's spouse, without the model, his own holy Mother, is to imagine that mere formulas and concepts are realities.[3]

In his sermon entitled "Jesus Entered," Meister Eckhart (d. 1327), a Rhenish Dominican mystic, evoked this feminine principle at work in all human beings in these bold words:

For a man to become fruitful he must be a wife. "Wife," here, is the noblest name that can be given to the mind, and it is indeed more noble than "virgin." That man should receive God in himself is good, and by this reception he is a virgin. But that God should become fruitful in him is better, for the fruitfulness of a gift is the only gratitude for the gift. The spirit is wife when in gratitude it gives birth in return and bears Jesus back into God's fatherly heart.[4]

In the same sermon Eckhart continued:

There is a power in the mind which touches neither time nor flesh; it emanates from the spirit and remains in the spirit and is totally spiritual. In this power, God is fully verdant and flowering, in all the joy and all the honor that he is in himself. There reigns such a dear joy, so incomprehensibly great a joy, that no one can ever fully speak of it. For in this power, the eternal Father is ceaselessly begetting his eternal Son, in such a way that this power begets the Son of God together with him and begets itself as this self-same Son in the identical power of the Father.[5]

The virgin birth of Christ is the greatest marvel and wonder of God. It was possible because Mary was totally open to God. The spiritual virgin birth of Christ is also possible *in each one* of us if we also open ourselves totally to God. Reflecting on this mystery, Dom Bede Griffiths wrote in *Return to the Center:*

> The virgin birth of Jesus is achieved because a woman is found who can make the total surrender of herself in love. What human love strives imperfectly to achieve through sex and marriage is here accomplished by divine Love. The mystery of love which is at work in the whole creation, in the stars and atoms, plants and animals and men, here achieved its consummation. In Mary man is married to God; the male and female unite in one person in an interior marriage and the new man is born. . . . The new man is not born by sexual generation: "Not of blood nor the will of the flesh nor the will of man, but of God" (John 1:13). This is the mystery which has to be accomplished in us. Every man and woman has to undergo this virgin birth, to be married to God. In other words, beyond our physical and psychic being we have to discover our spiritual being, our eternal ground, and there the mystery of love is fulfilled.[6]

If we allow ourselves to be free and disengaged from attachment to all things, we can experience this spiritual fruitfulness, the mystery of that "virgin ground" in us where the new man or woman is born out of the infinite fruitfulness of God. Jesus said, "I am the vine, you are the branches. The person who abides in me and I in that person, that one it is that bears much fruit" (John 15:5). Returning to Meister Eckhart's sermon, we hear:

> A virgin who is a wife, free and disengaged from attachment, is at all times equally close to God and to herself. She bears many fruits, which are big, neither more nor less than God himself. This virgin who is a wife produces this fruit and this birth, and she bears fruit, a hundred or thousand times a day, yes incessantly, by giving birth and by becoming fruitful from the most noble ground. To say it even better: truly, she is fruitful out of the same ground from which the Father begets his eternal Word, and she begets

together with him. For Jesus—the light and the reflection of the fatherly heart, as St. Paul says, he is an honor and a reflection of the father's heart, and his radiance shines through the father's heart with power—this Jesus is united to her, and she is united to him, and she shines and is resplendent with him, one identical unity, a pure and clear light in the father's heart.[7]

Is it true that we are *all* feminine in our relationship to God? As you reflect on your own contemplative experience, the truth of this dynamic may become apparent to you. I realize that there is a certain awkwardness in recommending to others that they become comfortable thinking of themselves in the role of Mary at the Annunciation, especially when many of my readers will be male. As we begin to move into a relationship of union with God, we must not be surprised when familiar attitudes receive a "shock" or a "jolt." New life is always a jolt to old ways of feeling, thinking, and being.

The crucifixion is probably the rudest jolt of all, but it is only the extension of Mary's *fiat:* "Be it done to me, according to your word." Meister Eckhart saw this "shock" and "jolt" as "an incomprehensibly great joy."[8]

### Mary, the Symbol of Total Humility

The centuries, the millennia, of preparation for the incarnation were clues to what the fullness of time would bring forth. Central to God's plan was a young woman, the one who would give Jesus all that is human.

When Mary was in prayer, sighing and beseeching God more fervently to send his people a Redeemer, the archangel Gabriel arrived, the bearer of good tidings. He entered and saluted her, saying, "Hail, most favored one; the Lord is with you; blessed are you among women!" (Luke 1:28).

How did Mary respond to this salutation? She remained silent, but, reflecting upon the angel's words, was unsettled by them. Her trouble arose entirely from her humility, which was disturbed at the sound of praises so far exceeding her own lowly estimate of herself. Gabriel, seeing Mary so troubled by the salutation, was obliged to encourage her, saying, "Fear not, Mary! for you have found grace with God. Listen! You are to conceive and bear a son, and you must name him Jesus. He will be great and will be called Son of the Most High. The Lord God will give him the throne of his ancestor David; he will rule over the House of Jacob forever and his reign will have no end" (Luke 1:30-33).

Mary said to the angel, "But how can this come about, since I am a virgin?"

"The Holy Spirit will come upon you," the angel answered, "and the power of the Most High will cover you with its shadow. And the child will be holy and will be called Son of God. Know this too: your kinswoman Elizabeth has, in her old age, herself conceived a son, and she whom people called barren is now in her sixth month, for nothing is impossible to God."

"I am the handmaid of the Lord," said Mary, "let what you have said be done to me." And the angel left her (Luke 1:26-38).

Oh, what more beautiful, more humble, more prudent answer which gives joy in heaven and brought an immense sea of grace and blessings into the world! In his first of the four sermons *In Praise of the Virgin Mary*, St. Bernard attributes the motherhood of Mary to her humility. His reasoning goes like this:

> You can be saved without virginity, but without humility you cannot be. Humility which deplores the loss of virginity can still find favor. Yet, I dare say that, without humility, not even Mary's virginity would have been acceptable. The Lord says, "Upon whom shall my Spirit rest, if not upon him that is humble and contrite in spirit?" (Isaiah 66:2). Note that he says, "on the humble," and

not "on the virgin." Had Mary not been humble, then, the Holy Spirit would not have rested upon her. Had the Spirit not rested upon her, she would not have become pregnant. How, indeed, could she have conceived by the Holy Spirit without him? It seems evident, then, that she conceived by the Holy Spirit because, as she herself said, "God regarded the lowliness of his handmaid," rather than her virginity. And even if it were because of her virginity that she found favor, she conceived, nevertheless, on account of her humility. Thus, there is no doubt that her virginity was found pleasing because her humility made it so.[9]

Anticipating a question on the meaning of the enjoyment of intimate union with Christ, or contemplative experience, Bernard insisted on the need of humility:

There may be someone who will ask me, "What does it mean to enjoy the Word?" I would answer that that one must find someone who has experience of it and ask that person. Do you suppose that if I had that experience I could describe it to you? . . . I may have been granted this experience but I do not speak of it. I have made allowance in what I have said, so that you could understand me. Oh, whoever is curious to know what it means to enjoy the Word, make ready your heart, not your ear! The tongue does not teach this, grace does. It is hidden from the wise and prudent and revealed to children. Humility, my brothers, is a great virtue, great and sublime. It can attain to what it cannot learn; it is counted worthy to possess what it has not the power to possess; it is worthy to conceive by the Word and from the Word, what it cannot explain in words. Why is this? Not because it deserves to do so, but because it pleases the Father of the Word, the Bridegroom of the soul, Jesus Christ our Lord who is God above all, blessed for ever. Amen.[10]

Humility is the key virtue of the contemplative path. Without it the most sublime and delicate mysteries of God, the intimate joys of union, are wasted in egotism and self-importance. The contemplative path can be dangerous. Souls can be destroyed by trying to drink from those holy wine casks of the intimate knowledge of God without first having grounded themselves in humility. The tradition insists on this, and this is why the tradition also insists so strongly that Mary's most important virtue is her humility. Once again she models the way we must be if we wish to receive the contemplative experience of intimate union with God.

As we proceed in our contemplative journey, we must proceed with humility, never being too proud to call upon Mary for help. In his sermon *Missus Est,* Bernard spoke beautifully about the power of the name of Mary, using the well-loved image of Mary as the "Star of the Sea":

> She—the Star shed on earth to warm our heart, fostering virtue and destroying vices. The splendid star wondrous suspended over the great wide sea. O you! Being tossed about, do not avert your eyes from this brightness of the Star. When wind of temptation blows up within, gaze up at this Star! Call out to Mary! When urge of fleshly desires are battering the skiff–small boat of your soul, call out to Mary. When your sins weigh you down, and you are bewildered by the loathsomeness of your conscience. When terrifying thought of judgment appalls you, and you begin to collapse in the gulf of sadness and despair. Gaze up to the Star. Call out to Mary. In danger, hardship, in every doubt, think of Mary. Call out to her! Keep her in your mouth, keep her in your heart. Follow the example of her life, and you will obtain the favor of her prayer. Follow her, you will never go astray. Asking her help, you will never despair. . . . Her kindness will see you to the end. Then you will know by your own experience how true it is that the Virgin Name was Mary–the Star of the Sea![11]

### *Mary, the Contemplative Flower*

In Eastern tradition, the flower is often used to express those aspects of spiritual insight that are too often delicate of nuance or too fragrant with beauty to be subjected to the harsh confinement of language and reasoning. Instead, the master will often simply sit before the disciples and hold up a single flower. There is an interesting anecdote heard in the Asian monastic circles entitled "Sakyamuni Holds Up a Flower." It goes like this:

> Long ago, when the World-Honored-One was at Mount Gradhraketa to give a talk, he held up a flower before the assembly. At this, all remained silent. The Venerable Kasho alone broke into a smile. The World-Honored-One then said, "I have the all-pervading True Dharma (namely, the Ultimate Truth). I now hand it on to Maha Kasho."[12]

Later, a famous poem was written, commenting on this incident:

> A Flower is held up
> And the secret has been revealed.
> Kasho breaks into a smile;
> The whole assemblage is at a loss.[13]

Now it is time to ask my readers: What, in your mind, is the "secret" of Sakyamuni holding up the flower, and why was it that there was only one among all those thousands in attendance who could grasp that secret? How about you? Do you understand the "secret"? You will indeed understand and not be among those who were at a loss, if you understand why it is that Mary, being the Mystical Rose, is the beloved of the Song of Songs, and why it is that she calls herself the Lily of the Valley. The mystery of Mary reflected within the depths of your own soul will lead you to your own contemplative experience. For you must know that you and I, all of us, are holding the eternal flower in our hand; or rather, we are the flower itself. Again, an old master, commenting on the "secret" of Sakyamuni holding up the flower, wrote:

The rain last night
Scattered the flowers.
Fragrant is the castle
Surrounded by running waters.[14]

Reflection on the mystery of Mary and careful attention to her as a contemplative and a woman chosen by God can be a wonderful means leading us to our own contemplative experience in the depths of our being. This is not just an attitude of another era or the devotion to a particular saint. Rather, it is a universal appeal. It applies equally to men and women, to all those who would know their contemplative experience. We have here a model of the action that goes on within each soul. In this action, each soul, as the negative polarity of being, increases self-awareness to the level of consciousness that belonged to the Virgin Mary. The womb of Mary is a powerful symbol of the "ground of our being," and as such it reveals to us our primeval hunger to embrace God. Thus, we have our own contemplative experience when we yield to the femininity of Mary within us.

# Living Water

ALTHOUGH I HAVE SHARED some simple insights on contemplative experience and the ways leading to it, one thing is sure: no one of us has control over our love for God or our life of contemplation. All the masters of both East and West insist on this, that the contemplative experience calls for a purity of heart and a faithful living out of one's state in life and requires great desire, humble prayer, and perseverance. St. Bernard describes the intensity of the great desire in the following passage:

> If any of us, like the holy prophet, finds it is good to cling to the Lord and—that I may make my meaning more clear—if any one of us is so filled with desire that we wish to depart and be with Christ, if we seek the Lord with a desire so intense, a thirst ever so burning and with an unflagging effort, we will certainly meet the Word in the guise of the Bridegroom on whatever day he shall come. At such an hour, we will find ourselves locked in the arms of Wisdom; we will experience how sweet the divine love is as it flows into our heart. Our desire will be given to us, even while we are still a pilgrim on this earth—though not in its fullness and only for a short time, a very short time.[1]

Desire is both the fuel and the nourishment of the contemplative experience. This holy desire is never satisfied with Unity Attained but only increases in its thirst the more richly it is favored. This is the dynamic that makes for perseverance and constancy of holy desire, no matter how daunting the obstacles or how delayed the coming of the Bridegroom.

Bernard uses the image of milk and the fullness of the breasts to describe the urgency of this prayer of desire or the touch of the Holy Spirit, which he calls the "kiss of the mouth." In a famous passage from his sermons on the Song of Songs, he wrote:

> So great is the potency of that holy kiss, that no sooner has the bride received it, than she conceives and her breasts grow rounded with the fruitfulness of conception, bearing witness, as it were, with this milky abundance. People with an urge to frequent prayer will have experience of what I say. Often enough, when we approach the altar to pray, our hearts are dry and lukewarm. But if we persevere, there comes an unexpected infusion of grace, and our breasts expand as it were, and our interior is filled with an overflowing of love. . . .[2]

This is startling imagery, but clearly Bernard does not blush to use it and he develops it with enthusiasm. The issue is so important and the stakes are so high that all propriety must be set aside in stretching the limits of language to more than it can bear if we are to convey even a trace of this gift of God's love for our soul.

If we turn to the Eastern masters, we see them stretching language in another direction, but with no less a sense of the extreme, and no less a consciousness of the relentless demands of the contemplative call. I am referring to the theme of "the Gateless Gate Barrier," which they use to talk about the great attraction of unlimited Truth. The heart of God is the "Gateless Gate," a limited barrier from the point of view of our finite capacity to desire, but infinite and unlimited from the point of view of how desirable is the one who beckons us. Here is Master Mumon's poem on the Gateless Gate:

> The Gateless Gate is the Great Tao.
> There are thousands of ways to it.
> If you pass through this Barrier,
> You may walk freely in the Universe.

Then Mumon goes on to comment on the poem:

> To pass through this barrier, a truly brave soul will plunge
> straight into the reality of the Gateless Gate, staking his whole
> life. He will never hesitate, no matter what the difficulty that may
> be involved. Nothing can interfere with the practice of such a
> brave Truth-seeker. If, on the contrary, he hesitates to take his life
> in his practice, he will miss it in an instant, just as if he were to
> catch a glimpse of a horse galloping past the window. He will lose
> sight of his contemplative experience and will never be able even
> to approach the Gate-of-no-gate.[3]

Clearly, we are not speaking of something that is investigated
philosophically or understood intellectually. This is concrete fact
that is experienced directly. It is the way of darkness. It is the way
of the most intense light. It is the way of the heart.

I have offered Bernard's, Tozan's, and my own humble path
with the hope that you will be helped to find your own way to
contemplative experience, that is, to an experiential realization of
intimate union with God in Christ.

The diagram on the following page serves as a synopsis of all
I have said. Reading the diagram horizontally, you will find on the
first line the five steps of Master Tozan Ryokai; on the second
line, pivotal texts from chapter 7 of the Song of Songs; and on
the third line, the five diagrams presented by D. T. Suzuki and
Eric Fromm.

If you care to try any of these ways, I would like to remind you
that the way to contemplative experience is a mystery to be contemplated and experienced, not an academic theory to be dis-

cussed. During your meditation and at all times you need to have a deep intuitive faith for Jesus to make himself present to you, and an intimate love to let him embrace you.

**The Five Steps Leading to Contemplative Experience**

| *Step 1* Guest in Host | *Step 2* Host in Guest | *Step 3* Resurgence | *Step 4* Inter- penetration | *Step 5* Unity Attained |
|---|---|---|---|---|
| I am my Beloved's. | My Beloved is mine. | Let's go to the field. | To see the vines' blossoms. | There I will give you my love. |
| A ⟶ B | B ⟵ A | A  B | A  B | |

If you wish to pass through the step of Unity Attained, first meditate on this verse of Master Tozan:

> How many times has Tokun,
> The idle old Gimlet,
> Not come down
> From that "Marvelous Peak!"
> He hires flush wise men
> And he and they together,
> Fill up the Well.[4]

Then, join the Holy Spirit to pray the prayer of St. John:

> Both the Spirit and the Bride say:
> "Amen. Come, Lord Jesus!" (Rev. 22:20)

The prayer of St. John and that of Master Tozan ardently raised will be fulfilled in the word of Jesus to the Samaritan woman:

The water that I shall give you
will become in you
A spring of water
welling up to eternal life. (John 4:14)

*Come, Lord Jesus!*

## PART FIVE

# Epilogue

# Living in the Company of the Blessed Trinity

"**G**OD IS LOVE," WRITES JOHN, the disciple whom Jesus loved. Since God is love, he is, as it were, lured by goodness and love to leave his dwelling place and come to abide with us. Wisdom speaks of herself:

> I was by his side,
> delighting him day after day,
> ever at play in his presence,
> at play everywhere in the world,
> delighting to be with the children of men.
> (Prov. 8:30–31)

Like Wisdom, I desire to live in the company of the Blessed Trinity, because I realize that the Trinity is living in the inmost depths of my being. To lead a contemplative life is nothing else than to live the actual presence of the Trinity. Every one of us, by the very fact that we exist, is always in the presence of the Trinity. This is especially true of the Christian people who have been called to know the ultimate secret of divine life, since by our baptism we have become sharers in the divine sonship of Jesus and thus part of the very life of God.

To live in the company of God should be as natural for us as to breathe the air that surrounds us. Furthermore, to live consciously in this company should never have for us the appearance of a duty we are bound to perform in obedience to some law. No, for me to live in the company of God is a birthright; it is the deepest aspiration of my nature, it is the spontaneous expression of my love for the Lord when I know that I am a child of God.

The Trinity is always present to me. There is no time or place in my daily life and work in which God is not in my company. There is no time or place in which God is more present to me or less present to me. God is always the same, the infinite, the eternal love. Everywhere and always he is; he is himself in his fullness. He enjoys forever the unspeakable bliss of his Presence to himself: the Presence of the Father to the Son, and the Son to the Father, and the mutual Presence of both to the Holy Spirit. This mystery is revealed to us by Jesus himself, out of his experience as Son of God.

How happy are we to have the privilege of being aware of this Presence and of being called to reciprocate it! That is, we are called to be in the company of God as God is in company with us. "Make your home in me," Jesus invites us, "as I make mine in you" (John 15:4). "If you love me," said Jesus, "you will keep my word, and my Father and I will come to make our home with you" (John 14:23).

To live in the company of the Trinity *is* our contemplative experience, our life of prayer. It is therefore not a special way of life reserved for those few individuals who are called to get away from the world and to dwell in the desert. To live in the company of the Trinity ought to be the very breath of every disciple of Christ. When we breathe, we do not say: "Let us *think* of the air that surrounds us and then breathe." Willingly, unwillingly, consciously, unconsciously, we breathe and go on breathing; continually too air is entering our lungs. So it is with the Presence that is more essential to our life, to our being, than the air itself that we breathe. Let us simply put ourselves in the presence of the Presence and adore!

Tertullian, a third-century Latin church father, used a spring of water as a symbol of the Trinity: the Father is the hidden source of the water; the Son is the river welling to the "peak"; the Holy Spirit is the irrigation that brings the water to all creation.

One of the lasting effects of my "moment" of contemplative experience, which I shared with you earlier, has been a glimpse into the mystery of the Trinity. At the moment the experience occurred I felt as if I were seeing before my eyes the Trinity as an immense ocean of love and of life. At some point during my experience—I do not know when—this immense ocean swelled and rose up to the Marvelous Peak. I felt the rising of this immense ocean to its peak as the Father begetting his Son. The Son—the Marvelous Peak—in turn poured himself down to the depths of the ocean. When this pouring down reached the "mysterious abyss," it became infinite bliss. I visualized this infinite bliss as the Holy Spirit. For my own sake I jotted this experience down in the form of a simple drawing and a few stanzas:

### The Trinity's Bliss

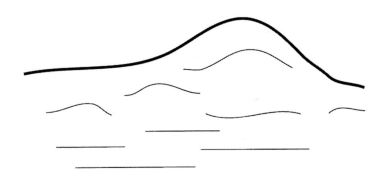

Being, Principle of Life, of Light and Goodness
Actualizes Self by pouring these out.
As this pouring reaches its "Marvelous Peak,"
The Only-Eternal Son is born.

Being eternally begotten from God,
The Son, in turn, pours Self all out.
When this pouring breaks down the unutterable Abyss,
The uncommunicable Bliss is "proceeding."

Being aware of Itself as the Love of Both,
The Eternal Bliss moves Self as divine Spirit,
Who joins the Begetting and Begotten together
In an ineffably piercing Embrace.

This is an eternally repeating Procession,
An ever-renewed-coming and ever-freshness;
It goes on within Self all at once,
Outside of time, and in spaceless sphere.

As God is like the Ocean of moving Delight,
The waves as seen as rising within It
Indicate man's measure of contemplative experience.
Those lying flat are ones still in deep sleep.

We must experience the intimate union
of Christ the Bridegroom and the Church his Bride
To realize within us
This Trinity's Bliss.

The mystery of the Trinity is inexhaustible, and no single for-
mulation can fully convey its meaning and its depths. We certainly need to dig into our theology in order to be guided in our
thinking and praying. But here there is no question of an academic learning. It is rather a matter of awakening, of awareness far
beyond the reach of our intellect, and an experience that springs
up and erupts in the deepest recesses of our being.

So long as our eyes have not been unsealed by faith, we are absolutely incapable of receiving that revelation in our mind or that experience in our heart. The experience of the Trinity carries the soul to the very center, the very source of its being. When that blessed time comes that we penetrate the heart of the Trinity and experience our "connaturality" with God, the Spirit of Wisdom makes known to us some secrets of the life of the Trinity.

To live in the company of the Trinity *is* our contemplative experience. The more intimate the company, the deeper the experience.

# Notes

**Part One: Contemplative Experience**

*Chapter 1*
*What Is Contemplative Experience?*

1. *The Letters of St. Bernard of Clairvaux,* trans. B. S. James (London: Burn & Oates, 1958) Letter 107, p. 156.

2. D. T. Suzuki and Erich Fromm, *Zen Buddhism and Psychoanalysis* (New York: Harper & Row, 1960), p. 2.

3. Jean Daniélou, *The Presence of God,* trans. Walter Robert (London: A. R. Mowbray, 1958), p. 12.

4. Philip Sheldrake, *Befriending Our Desires* (Notre Dame, Ind.: Ave Maria Press, 1994), p. 70.

5. Isshu Miura and Ruth Fuller Sasaki, *The Zen Koan* (New York: Harcourt Brace, 1965), p. 49.

*Chapter 3*
*Erotic Love and Spiritual Union*

1. Mishna *Yadayim* 3:5, as quoted in Rabbi Joseph Telushkin, *Jewish Wisdom* (New York: William Morrow, 1994), p. 129.

2. Clifford Stevens, *Intimacy with God* (Schuyler, Neb.: BMH Publications, 1992), p. 111.

3. Bernard McGinn, *The Foundations of Mysticism* (New York: Crossroad, 1992), p. 118.

4. Ibid., p. 26.

5. C. S. Lewis, *The Four Loves* (New York: Harcourt, 1960), pp. 150–51.

6. Rollo May, *Love and Will* (New York: Dell, 1969), pp. 71–72.

7. Denys Turner, *Eros and Allegory: Medieval Exegesis on the Song of Songs* (Kalamazoo, Mich.: Cistercian Publications, 1995), p. 20.

8. Origen, *Commentary on the Song of Songs*, trans. R. P. Lawson (Westminster, Md.: Newman Press, 1957), pp. 23–24.

9. McGinn, *Foundations of Mysticism*, p. 118.

10. Origen, *Commentary*, p. 35.

11. Denys Turner, *Eros and Allegory*, pp. 217ff.

12. McGinn, *Foundations of Mysticism*, p. 260.

13. *The Writings of St. Augustine*, Vol. 1, *Soliloquies*, trans. Thomas Gillian (New York: CIMA, 1948), chap. 4, pp. 372–73.

14. McGinn, *Foundations of Mysticism*, p. 260.

15. Turner, *Eros and Allegory*, p. 25.

## Part Two: A Holy Desire

### Chapter 4
### Moving toward a Holy Desire

1. Rollo May, *Love and Will* (New York: Dell, 1969), pp. 71–72.

2. C. S. Lewis, *The Four Loves* (New York: Harcourt, 1960) pp. 150–51.

3. Bernard McGinn, *Foundations of Mysticism* (New York: Crossroad, 1992), p. 120.

4. Origen, *Commentary on the Song of Songs*, trans. R. P. Lawson (Westminster, Md: Newman Press, 1957), p. 36.

5. McGinn, *Foundations of Mysticism*, pp. 120–21.

6. St. John Climacus, *The Ladder of Divine Ascent*, 5th Step (28) p. 57, as quoted in Oliver Clement, *The Roots of Christian Mysticism* (Hyde Park, N.Y.: New City Press, 1995), p. 175.

7. St. Gregory of Nyssa, *Commentary on the Song of Songs*, trans. Casmir McCambley, O.C.S.O. (Brookline, Mass.: Hellenic College, 1987), p. 49.

### Chapter 5
### The Eucharist

1. Caryll Houselander, *The Reed of God* (New York: Sheed & Ward, 1944), p. 84.

2. St. Gregory of Nyssa, *Homilies on the Song of Songs 10*, trans. Casmir McCambley, O.C.S.O. (Brookline, Mass.: Hellenic College, 1987), p. 193.

3. George Maloney, "Introduction," in Frank Tuoti, *Why Not Be a Mystic?* (New York: Crossroad, 1995), p. 16.

### Chapter 6
### Suffering Love

1. Origen, *Commentary on the Song of Songs,* trans. R. P. Lawson (Westminster, Md.: Newman Press, 1957), p. 198.

### Chapter 7
### Sacred Reading

1. *Catechism of the Catholic Church,* trans. United States Catholic Conference (Boston: Pauline Books & Media, 1994), #2705.

2. Origen, *Letter to Gregory Thaumaturgus* 3, as quoted in Oliver Clement, *The Roots of Christian Mysticism* (Hyde Park, N.Y.: New City Press, 1995), p. 100.

3. John Cassian, *The Conferences,* trans. Boniface Ramsey (New York: Paulist Press, 1997), *Conference 14,* p. 519.

4. André Louf, "Scientific Exegesis or Monastic Lectio," *Collectanea* 22 (July–September 1960): 236ff.

5. St. Bernard of Clairvaux, *Sermones super Cantica canticorum* (= *SC*), 23:3, trans. Kilian Walsh, Cistercian Fathers Series (CF) 7 (Kalamazoo, Mich.: Cistercian Publications, 1976).

6. *SC* 73:2; CF 40 (1980) 76.

7. *SC* 16:1; CF 4 (1971) 114.

8. St. Bernard of Clairvaux, *Sermo in Dominica IV post Pentecostem, Sermon for the Fourth Sunday after Pentecost,* in *Seasons and Principal Festivals of the Year,* trans. monk of Mount Melleray Abbey (Westminster, Md.: Carroll Press, 1950), p. 55.

### Chapter 8
### Reading Scripture as Reading a Zen Koan

1. William Johnston, *Christian Zen* (New York: Harper & Row, 1971), p. 63.

### Part Three: Steps Leading to Contemplative Experience

### Chapter 10
### Contemplative Experience according to
### St. Bernard and Master Tozan Ryokai

1. Etienne Gilson, *Dante the Philosopher* (New York: Crossroad, 1949), p. 48.

2. Isshu Miura and Ruth Fuller Sasaki, *The Zen Koan* (New York: Harcourt Brace, 1965), pp. 67–72.

### Chapter 11
### Step One: Guest in Host Experience

1. Isshu Miura and Ruth Fuller Sasaki, *The Zen Koan* (New York: Harcourt Brace, 1965), pp. 67ff. Citations from Master Tozan are from this work.

2. D. T. Suzuki and Erich Fromm, *Zen Buddhism and Psychoanalysis* (New York: Harper & Row, 1960), pp. 65ff. Other references to D. T. Suzuki and Erich Fromm are to this work.

3. *SC* 14:6; CF 4:102.

### Chapter 12
### Step Two: Host in Guest

1. Carl Kopf, *Window of Life*, ed. Charles L. Wallis, in *A Treasure of Sermon Illustrations* (New York: Abingdon Press, 1950), p. 18.

2. Elie Wiesel, *Souls on Fire: Portraits and Legends of Hasidic Masters* (New York: Random House, 1972), pp. 203–6.

3. *SC* 36:6; CF 7:179.

4. *SC* 50:6; CF 31 (1979) 35f.

### Chapter 13
### Step Three: The Resurgence of the Host

1. John Tauler, *Spiritual Conferences*, trans. Eric Colledge (St. Louis: Herder Book Co., 1961), p. 156.

2. *SC* 31:7; CF 7:129.

3. *SC* 85:13; CF 40:209f.

4. *SC* 85:13; CF 40:209f.

### Chapter 14
### Step Four: Mutual Interpenetration
### of Guest and Host

1. St. Bernard of Clairvaux, *Missus Est* 3.2 in *Seasons and Principal Festivals of the Year*, trans. monk of Mount Melleray Abbey (Westminster, Md.: Carroll Press, 1950, 1:55ff.

2. *SC* 67:8; CF 40:12.

3. *SC* 83:3; CF 40:182f..

4. Zenkei Shibayama, *Zen Comments on the Mumonkan*, trans. Sumiko Kudo (New York: New American Library, 1975), p. 43.

5. Ibid.

6. Ibid., p. 50.

7. Ibid., p. 229.

8. *SC* 31:6; CF 7:129.

9. St. Bernard of Clairvaux, *Sermon 1*, in *Seasons and Principal Festivals*, 1:1ff.

## Chapter 15
### *Step Five: Unity Attained*

1. Ernest Wood, *Soto*, in *Zen Dictionary* (Tokyo: Charles Tuttle, 1972), p. 129.

2. Lao Tzu, *Tao-te-Ching* (New York: Bobbs-Merrill, 1968), p. 176.

3. *SC* 85:13; CF 40:209.

4. *SC* 1:11: CF 4:6f.

5. St. Bernard of Clairvaux, *De Diligendo Deo* (*Dil.*) 10:27, trans. Robert Walton, *On Loving God*, CF 13 (1974) 119.

6. Ibid.

7. *SC* 52:6; CF 31:54.

8. *SC* 52:3; CF 31:52.

9. *SC* 52:4; CF 31:52.

10. *SC* 85:13; CF 40:209.

11. Etienne Gilson, *The Mystical Theology of St. Bernard*, trans. A. H. Downes (London: Sheed & Ward, 1955), p. 80.

12. *Dil.* 9; CF 13:101.

13. *Dil.* 8; CF 13:100.

14. *Dil.* 7; CF 13:100.

15. *SC* 83:6; CF 40:186.

16. *SC* 85:14; CF 40:210.

17. D. T. Suzuki, *Zen Buddhism*, ed. William Barrett (New York: Doubleday, 1956), p. 107.

## Part Four: Contemplative Experience and Beyond

### Chapter 16
### Contemplative Experience and the Active Life

1. William of St. Thierry, *Vita Bernardi*, in Migne, *PL* 185:238ff.

2. *SC* 57:9; CF 31:103.

3. Bernard McGinn, *The Growth of Mysticism* (New York: Crossroad, 1994), p. 76.

4. *SC* 57:9; CF 31:104.

### Chapter 17
### Mary, the Model of Contemplative Experience

1. George Maloney, *Mary the Womb of God* (Denville, N.J.: Dimension Books, 1976), pp. 21–22.

2. L. Beirnaert, *Mystique et Conscience* (Paris, 1952), pp. 377, as quoted in Maloney, *Mary the Womb of God*, p. 21.

3. Matthew Kelty, *Flute Solo* (New York: Image Books, 1980), p. 106.

4. Reiner Schurmann, *Meister Eckhart: Mystic and Philosopher* (Bloomington: Indiana University Press, 1978), p. 4.

5. Ibid., p. 5.

6. Bede Griffiths, *Return to the Center* (Springfield, Ill.: Templegate, 1977), pp. 64–65.

7. Schurmann, *Meister Eckhart*, p. 58.

8. Ibid., p. 5.

9. Bernard of Clairvaux, *Magnificat in Praise of the Blessed Virgin Mary*, trans. Marie Bernard, Cistercian Fathers Series 18 (Kalamazoo, Mich.: Cistercian Publications, 1979), pp. 9–10.

10. *SC* 85:14; CF 40:210.

11. *Sermon 3*, in *Seasons and Principal Festivals of the Year*, trans. monk of Mount Melleray Abbey (Westminster, Md.: Carroll Press, 1950), 1:91.

12. Zenkei Shibayama, *Zen Comments on the Mumonkan*, trans. Sumiko Kudo (New York: New American Library, 1975), p. 59.

13. Ibid., p. 9.

14. Ibid., p. 7.